Winning Styles for Winning Coaches

Creating the Environment for Victory

Kay McGuire

Sagamore Publishing, Inc.
Champaign, IL

© 1992 Sagamore Publishing Co., Inc.

Except for appropriate use in critical reviews, the reproduction or use of this work in any form or by any electronic or mechanical means now known or hereafter invented, including photocopying and recording, or in any information storage and retrieval system is forbidden without the written permission of the publisher.

Book design: Brian J. Moore
Cover, graphics: Michelle R. Dressen
Editor: Joyce D. Meyer
Proofreader: Phyllis L. Bannon

10 9 8 7 6 5 4 3 2 1

Library of Congress Catalog Card Number: 91-67443
ISBN: 0-915611-49-x

Sagamore Publishing Co., Inc.
P.O. Box 673
Champaign, IL 61824-0673

Printed in the United States of America

To Dick, Dona, Cam and Dad with my love
and thanks for your love, patience, understanding,
and encouragement of me.

Contents

- Acknowledgments vii
- Introduction ix
1. It's a Matter of Style 1
2. "D" is for Dominance 17
3. "I" is for Interaction 35
4. "S" is for Steadiness 57
5. "C" is for Cautious Compliance 77
6. Chemistry in Action 95
7. Non-Verbal Cues 113
8. Communicating with Style 123
9. Winning Over Stress 139
10. Creating a Winning Environment 151
- Epilogue 165
- References 167

Acknowledgments

When you begin to acknowledge the people who have been an important part of your work, it is hard to separate the personal from the professional. The first person to encourage me to do what I was best at — which in his mind was anything I wanted to do — was my Dad, the late Charles W. Clabaugh. He introduced me to sports, to public speaking, working with people, and to the joy of reading. Each of these elements has been very important to me in my professional and personal life.

My husband, Dick McGuire, who has always loved me, listened to me, and encouraged me to grow has been my best friend for almost 30 years and is the best "sounding board" in the world. I want to thank our daughter Dona for introducing me to women's sports. She participated in sports in high school and introduced me to a wider horizon in sports than I had been aware of. She also was helpful at home and understanding when I had to be "on the road" as my speaking and training career grew. She is also my best friend. To our new son-in-law, Cam Pepper, I want him to know that he is a very welcome addition to our family. He also has given me additional perspective on sports and the sense of team from his experience while playing football for the University of Illinois and in the World Football League.

I would not have been able to have the first hand experience or knowledge to transfer this information from the business and educational environment had it not been for Dr. Mike Hebert and his women's volleyball program at the University of Illinois. Mike, along with his staff and teams encouraged me, acted as guinea pigs, and gave me invaluable feedback as we first used this information with sports teams. Thanks to Mike and his wife Sherry for becoming valuable personal and professional friends.

Thanks also to Dr. Karol Kahrs, associate athletic director at the University of Illinois for her personal and professional encouragement. She encouraged me as I began working with a variety of sports, both men's and women's teams, and national groups.

Although the focus of this book is for coaches of athletic teams, I use the material in all areas of my training and consulting business. The skills for understanding people and working together as a team transcend all areas of our lives. I first worked with educational groups and had tremendous encouragement and help from my good friend Marilyn Holt — thanks for all you have done. Many people in business have given me advice and encouragement as well as hired me to work with their organization. Also thanks to all the persons that have participated in my programs — you have made all of this happen.

A special thanks to Patricia Welling who introduced me to the Personal Profile System. To all the people at Carlson Learning Company, staff and associates around the country who are always willing to help and share information. To Jack, Joan, Alice, Lynne, Sandy, Jeannie, Michael, Gary, Diane, and Gene — thanks for encouragement, listening, supporting and caring. To each of you who reads this book, I'm excited that you want to learn new skills for working with people. As I say at the conclusion of a presentation on this subject, "I encourage each of you to live life to the fullest and do it with style!!"

Introduction

Some coaches live by Vince Lombardi's motto:
"Winning isn't everything; it's the only thing."

Others believe in Grantland Rice's formulation:
"When the One Great Scorer comes to write against your name — He marks — not that you won or lost — but how you played the game."

Neither philosophy is entirely satisfying to the lover of athletic competition.

If winning were the only thing, then organized sports would be a no-holds-barred affair. Steroids would be in; Marquess of Queensbury rules would be out. The spitball would be an accepted stratagem. The NCAA's recruiting regulations would be hooted away. College coaches could go after the best and the meanest, no matter how many Mercedeses and BMWs the alumni had to cough up to get them.

Thank goodness, that isn't the way most fans like their sports.

But neither will they sit in drafty gyms, windswept stadiums or sun-baked bleachers to watch a team whose objective is not victory, but some undefinable quality that makes it look good in victory or defeat.

When two teams take to the field or arena, one of them is expected to emerge victorious. The fans didn't flock to Yankee Stadium to watch Babe Ruth's form in batting practice or to admire Lou Gehrig's character. They went to watch Murderer's Row butcher opposing pitchers on the way to pennants and World Series.

They didn't go to the arena to watch Muhammad Ali float like a butterfly. They went hoping to see him knock his opponent out—or be knocked out himself. When the Cornhuskers of Nebraska square off against the Sooners of Oklahoma, nobody is happy with a tie, even if the standoff is regarded as a "moral victory" for one of the teams.

The object of entering athletic competition should be to win: to win honestly and fairly, observing all the niceties of sportsmanship, to be sure. But the coach who doesn't go into a season with the intention of winning as many games as possible is the coach who ends up with mediocre seasons at best and, eventually, no contract.

As Penn State Coach Joe Paterno (1989) put it:

> I love winning football games as much as any coach. My players love winning. Without that, Penn State teams couldn't have come out winners season after season or win national championships. But we also draw on an underlying layer of strength and power that gives us an advantage: While committing everything we've got to playing our best game, we know there's something that counts for more than winning. (p. 17)

Learning to lose may build character, but so does learning to win. We all lose now and then, but winning is always more comfortable, especially when we know the victory was hard-earned.

This book is directed toward the coach who wants to win while promoting the human values that, no matter what the undertaking, will make winning worthwhile. It will not teach athletic strategy or technique; that's not my field.

Let's start from a premise that every coach recognizes as valid: Athletic ability is only the beginning of the formula for victory. Talented teams can go 0-30 for the season. To win consistently, a team needs a winning edge. That edge can be motivation — the desire and the will to win — together with teamwork. Motivation itself can arise from a thing we call chemistry: that precise blending of personalities, egos and aspirations that results in a smooth-functioning organization both on and off the field.

Good coaches know that a team is like a piece of machinery. You can build it from the finest parts in the world, but if they don't fit you've got trouble.

The key is in finding that "fit." Some coaches find it instinctively; they have a knack for putting together the right staff and the right athletes. They seem to know how to help the temperamental loner contribute to the team effort; how to turn the passive brooder into a tower of strength in the line-up; how to turn the off-the-field cut-up into an inspirational leader on the field.

The coach who has that intuitive talent is a lucky individual. The rest of us need help.

Fortunately, there's a way to take much of the guesswork out of team building and staff relationships. It's possible because human beings, as a group, are quite predictable. While each of us is a unique individual, we share a common humanity, and our human traits can be classified. With the help of some simple exercises, we can determine the behavior style of each person with whom we deal. Once we know that, we can predict how such persons will respond in given situations. We can understand what motivates them, what turns them off and how they fit into a cooperative framework. We can learn to dampen the petty jealousies, grudges and feuds that often undermine team spirit. We can turn squabblers into hustlers; losers into winners.

The formula is amazingly simple. It has been used successfully in business and industry for many years. I have used it in training sessions with business people ranging from corporate presidents through middle management to support staffs.

Then I began applying the system to athletic departments. I started with the University of Illinois volleyball team and the women's basketball team. The results were so impressive that I was asked to work with the men's tennis team and to conduct workshops for the overall coaching staff. I have since gone on to build a very successful consulting and training practice.

As one coach expressed it, "It's a remarkably practical experience." Armed with knowledge about the behavior patterns of each athlete, the coach can provide the motivation, training and discipline needed to turn a group of individuals into a winning team.

This book will use real-life examples involving many athletes and coaches from several different sports. The reader should be mindful that when a person is cited as an example of a particular behavior style, the categorization is not based on actual testing or observation, but on anecdotal material from that person's life. We cannot say, for instance, that Henry Aaron follows the S behavior style; we can only say that in the episodes cited, he showed the characteristics of that style.

For an authoritative, in-depth analysis of each player's behavior style, one would need to use instruments such as the Performax Personal Profile System, which I have used in my consulting work with athletic teams.

Detailed discussions of each of the behavior styles mentioned in this book may be found in the book *People Smart* by Tony Alessandra, Ph.D., and Michael J. O'Connor, Ph.D., with Janice Alessandra (Keynote Publishing Company, La Jolla, California). *People Smart* may be purchased through the Center for Creative Communication in Savoy, Illinois.

1

It's a Matter of Style

Yogi Berra was known as a bad-ball hitter. Every ball coming in from the mound was a juicy temptation to him. When it crossed the plate within shouting distance of the strike zone, Yogi would go for it. Though Yogi was a dangerous hitter, opposing pitchers knew that the bad ball was his weakness, and they tried to exploit it.

Early in Berra's career, Yankee manager Bucky Harris decided Yogi would be a much greater asset to the line-up if he would learn to let the bad ones go by.

"Think before you swing," he told his unorthodox catcher. Yogi tried to please his manager. He stood thoughtfully at the plate while the first pitch zipped over for a strike. He waited in deep contemplation as the second pitch passed him in the strike zone. He was positively cerebral as the umpire called him out on the third pitch.

Yogi returned to the dugout in frustration and groused to his manager, "How can a guy think and hit at the same time?" (Thorn, 1976, pp. 148-49).

In retrospect, one can see the futility of what Harris was trying to do. A Ted Williams wouldn't have to be told to think at the plate. He was, by nature, a student of the game. He was also a perfectionist who became a master of his craft. Berra was an easygoing guy who liked to play baseball, and he did it quite well if you didn't make him think about it at the plate. Each was a great player in his own way. Each achieved greatness by following his own particular behavior style.

Why would a strategy work for Ted Williams and flop for Yogi Berra? Because the two players followed different behavior styles. They responded to challenges, praise, criticism and instruction in different ways.

DIFFERENT STROKES...

Joe Paterno (1989) recalls approaching Coach Rip Engle once when Engle was head coach at Penn State and Paterno was his assistant.

"How can that kid have such a different outlook on football than that other kid from the same high school, same football program?" he asked. "How can he be so gung ho to practice while that other kid can't get himself out of first gear?"

Engle responded: "Joe, the longer you're in this business, the more you're going to realize that everybody's different." Paterno says he eventually learned, through trial and error, the different ways to handle different people (p. 84).

A good coach can sharpen intuition to such a point that he or she knows instinctively how to vary approaches to different personalities. Bela Karolyi, the great gymnastics coach, had to deal in different ways with Nadia Comaneci, the serious, perfectionist Romanian, and Mary Lou Retton, the bubbly, enthusiastic West Virginian. But he turned them both into Olympic champions. He realized he had to protect the introverted Comaneci from the unwanted glare of media attention and he had to calm Retton's effervescence in the interest of consistency (Retton and Karolyi, 1976, p. 10).

Karolyi's insight helped him see the difference between the two athletes and their respective needs. But none of us is intuitive enough to read other people perfectly, and all of us can benefit from a system that takes much of the guesswork out of the task.

WE'RE DIFFERENT BUT ALIKE

Whether you're looking at an assembly of executives in a board room, a crew of workers on a factory floor or a team of athletes in a locker room, you're looking at an assortment of personalities.

Each of Earth's five billion or so inhabitants is a unique individual who responds to the environment in an individualistic way. But each of us is also a member of the human race, drawing our characteristics from a bag of traits common to our species. We combine these traits in different proportions, but these combinations produce a limited number of behavior styles that can be identified and classified.

If you can group your athletes into a few behavior categories and learn what works with each of those categories, you can give yourself a decisive edge.

As Billy Martin (1987) put it:

> There is more to managing than filling out the lineup card and bringing in a new pitcher. There are relationships with the players, front office relationships, evaluating talent, knowing human nature, knowing when to push a team and when to back off. (p. 4)

Ed Temple (1980), coach of the renowned Tigerbelles of Tennessee State and of American women's Olympic runners, put it more colorfully: "A mule you drive, but with a race horse you use finesse" (p. 94).

Whether you're trying to relate to an administrator, a staff member, a star performer, or an underachieving athlete, it helps to know whether you're dealing with a race horse, a mule or some other type of fauna.

RAH-RAH VS. HERE'S HOW

During a workshop I conducted at the University of Illinois, volleyball coach Mike Hebert learned that different athletes require different approaches. Mike recalled a time-out pep talk he gave to his women's team. It was full of rah-rah motivation. Some of the players returned to the court all charged up and ready to win. Others seemed unmoved by his speech. During the workshop, his players told him why.

When Mike does his cheerleading bit, said one player, "I just roll my eyes and look at the crowd, because that doesn't mean anything to me. But when he can tell me specifically what I need to do in this situation then I relate."

"Oh, that's boring," responded another player. "I don't want to hear that. I want to come into the huddle and have Mike really say, 'Come on, gang! You can do it! You can do it! You can do it!'"

The two players heard Hebert's pep talk through different behavioral filters. One was a person who thrived on applause and acclaim; the rah-rahs worked for her. The other was a perfectionist whose motivation sprang from within. She didn't need a pep talk; she needed someone to tell her what to do to improve her performance.

Another Illinois coach was a person who took commitments seriously.

"If someone says to me, 'You made a commitment to do thus and so,' I will say 'You're right,' and I'll go ahead and fulfill that commitment," he said during a workshop conducted by me. But his players saw life through a different lens:

> They don't understand what you mean by a commitment to principles. If I say, "Get the ball from here to there," they understand. I thought they already knew that. Yet they need to hear it bit by bit, piece by piece. For me to tell them during time-out, "Look, you committed yourself to play hard tonight," is nonsense. They don't know what I'm talking about.

This coach had acquired a valuable insight: He learned that what he says isn't the only important factor in motivation. It's also important to consider to whom he's saying it and how that person perceives his message. To know that, he needs to know something about the behavioral lenses through which his players view the world.

All of us can think of coaches and athletes with contrasting styles. Babe Ruth was quite different from Joe DiMaggio. DiMaggio was different from Pete Rose. Charlie Hustle was no Ted Williams.

Among coaches and managers, Vince Lombardi and Tom Landry had different styles. Alabama's Bear Bryant was different from Penn State's Joe Paterno. Casey Stengel was a contrast with Joe McCarthy; Bobby Knight with Pat Riley; Leo

Durocher with Connie Mack, and Billy Martin with Tom Lasorda.

Lombardi and the Redskins

In his last season as a coach — with the demoralized Washington Redskins — Vince Lombardi seemed to be driven by the need to produce a winner overnight. We now know that the great coach was, in fact, running out of time. He would not live to coach another team.

Lombardi took over the team from the easygoing Otto Graham and drove it with a ruthlessness that sometimes bordered on cruelty. There was no time to adjust his approach to the individual behavior styles represented on the squad.

The approach worked with some players. Vincent Promuto, a guard who had played for Lombardi in Green Bay, responded positively to his old mentor:

> You see, some guys feel they're only doing what he wants them to do to keep from being yelled at. They're losers. You have to make one more step and see that it's not him that's making you play better football, but yourself. That's a feeling worth having. (Dowling, 1970, pp. 68-69)

Another player responded angrily:

> He motivates through fear. It's a terrible feeling to know you're afraid of the man you work for, terrible. When I think what I have gone through this year! The hell you go through making the team, and it was hell. And then the fear of having that taken away from you. The statements he makes when you're hurt, like if you don't play for me hurt I'll get rid of you. I've heard him tell that to people. Hell, he's told it to me. (Dowling, 1970, pp. 68-69)

Lombardi's tough methods turned off some team members, but Graham's nice-guy approach had not been universally applauded either. Many of the players had longed for a tough taskmaster to whip the team into shape.

While Graham was coach, one veteran had told his teammates:

You guys are just stupid if you don't go out there and win for Otto. You'll never have it so good again. Otto'll let us do anything we want, and if we win for the guy, he's going to be around for a long time. We can play this game for 10 years on Easy Street if you guys put out for Otto. (Dowling, 1970, pp. 127-28)

Lombardi was a tyrannical taskmaster who followed his own style, come what may. His players had better learn to adjust to it or look somewhere else for employment. Graham was a non-confrontational person who wanted to be liked. In Graham's final season with the 'Skins, they finished 5-9. Lombardi drove them to a 7-5 finish — an improvement, but hardly the stuff from which the Lombardi legend was forged.

Had Lombardi had the time to construct a team to his exacting specifications, as he had at Green Bay, he might have produced another series of winners. But in the fall of 1969, he took over a disheartened assortment of men following a variety of behavior styles. Perhaps sensing that time was running out for him, he seems to have made no effort to tailor his methods to the material on hand (Dowling, 1970, pp. 127-28). The result was a mediocre year for a mediocre team.

Obviously, tough methods work with some players while others respond to a more easygoing coaching style. Graham's methods as the Redskins' coach were no more productive than Lombardi's. Sometimes a team responds more positively to the tough methods of a dominating personality.

In 1982, when George Halas, owner of the Chicago Bears, was searching for someone to bring the Bears out of hibernation, it wasn't Mike Ditka's easygoing temperament that got him the job. Halas was looking for that tough taskmaster. One story has it that Halas was watching on television as the Bears played the Dallas Cowboys. Ditka was then assistant coach for Dallas. At one point in the game the camera zoomed in on Ditka, who was storming and raging on the sidelines. Halas decided this was the type of temperament needed to turn the Teddy Bears into Grizzlies. Ditka was hired, and sportscaster Tom Brooksheir, former defensive back for the Philadelphia Eagles, predicted Mike would instill a new intensity into the team. "The players will have to pay to get to the water bucket," he said (Stamborski, 1988, p. 8).

Ditka's dominating, blustering style put the Bears on the championship trail.

Would a more flexible Lombardi, more responsive to the varieties of human behavior, have achieved better results with the Redskins? It's hard to argue with the Lombardi record and the Lombardi legend. The great coach was a superlative example of what we shall refer to as the Dominance, or D, behavior style. So is Mike Ditka. Only about 15 percent of the population follows that style. Otto Graham's style fits the description of the S style — the "S" standing for Steadiness. This style also can be followed to success in the coaching field. The key to success is not in the style you follow but in your understanding of your own style and the behavior styles of your players.

You Don't Have to Be Lombardi

You don't have to be a Vince Lombardi to coach winners. You don't have to have that single-minded drive to bend a team of athletes to your will. Furthermore, if you're coaching scholastic sports, you don't have the option of trading and drafting players until you have just the team you want.

In most situations, your success will depend upon your ability to teach, motivate and lead athletes, either those you've recruited or those who simply show up at your gym, court or practice field.

TEAM CHEMISTRY

"It's important to have a certain chemistry on a baseball team, to have players who have played together for a few years and who know each other intimately, on the field and off," wrote Billy Martin (1987, pp. 147-48).

Most coaches don't have the luxury of several years to get to know their players; neither do their players have years in which to know each other intimately. So it would be helpful if coaches and players could find a formula that would help them know quickly what to expect from teammates and coaches.

If we can categorize human behavior into a few styles, learn the characteristics of those styles and then learn what style each player and coach follows, we can quickly gain the intimate knowledge that ordinarily would be acquired over a period of years.

Bill Perkins (1989), a Baptist minister who has coached soccer, baseball and basketball in his Oregon community, made this observation:

> I had only been coaching a short while when I learned that what helped one kid often hurt another. I quickly saw that understanding both my own personality and the different personalities of children was critical for effective parenting and coaching. (pp. 18-19)

The same principle works when dealing with associates on the coaching staff. If you ignore the behavior style of the person with whom you're dealing, you're not going to be effective in dealing with that person.

What's a Behavior Style?

All of us have our individual behavior styles. A behavior style is the way we think, feel and act. Our behavior pattern is linked to our personal identity: who we are.

Our friends can identify us by our physical appearances, by our voices and by the way we walk because these characteristics remain stable over time. Even when age adds wrinkles and pounds, there's a basic structure and pattern of movement that tells acquaintances who we are even if they have not seen us for several years. Our vocal characteristics usually follow us through life too. The listener who hears a youthful voice singing "I'll Be Seeing You" to the accompaniment of the big-band sound of the '40s will recognize the voice of the same Frank Sinatra who, as an aging crooner, sang "I Did It My Way."

In the same way, our core behavior remains stable over time. It's our instinctive way of responding to situations, and if it changes, it changes very slowly. Our behavior may change abruptly when we're under pressure, but that simply means that we have one style for ordinary circumstances and another when the heat is on. We also may alter our behavior in response to changing environments, just as the aging fast-ball pitcher who loses his speed will develop a knuckleball, slider and other pitches to compensate.

Billy Martin (1987) claimed he had a different behavior on the field from the one he followed off the field. He wrote:

> It's like a mask comes over my face when I go to the ballpark. I don't know how it ever came about, but it happens. As soon as I get out of that car and walk to the ballpark, I become another person. (p. 232)

Here's an example:

> I'm not a person who has ever been a perfectionist when it comes to neatness and order. In fact, I'm a bit of a slob at times. Now, all of a sudden, at the ballpark, as a manager, I become a perfectionist. Don't ask me why. (Martin, 1987, p. 232)

The reason is that Billy found it helpful to adapt his behavior style to the different conditions on the field. For the same reason, coaches who first encounter an athlete in a classroom setting may find they're dealing with a "different person" in the gym or on the practice field.

It's not a freakish phenomenon. Martin observed it with New York Yankees owner George Steinbrenner, in whom he saw at least six contrasting styles of behavior, and with sportscaster Howard Cosell:

> There's one Howard Cosell who's the public figure on the tube and there's another — a very private Howard Cosell — whom you meet in a bar and have a drink with. I think they are two different people. One he stages and becomes and the other is the natural Howard Cosell. (Martin, 1987, pp. 231-32)

John McEnroe's aggressive, abusive style on the tennis court is not replicated in his private life, according to his biographer, Richard Evans (1982):

> It is a shame his public cannot see Himself as Himself, to use an Irishism. Because Himself is not at all the kind of fellow you see projected through a television screen. So often his behavior invites his critics to see him as a loner, a man against the world, an aloof and cantankerous superstar with no more than a couple of close friends. Even on tour, where McEnroe does indeed have a few

enemies, that loner image is something of a joke among the other players, who find him an agreeable and amusing locker-room companion. (p. 19)

Casey Stengel was another multi-faceted individual. There was the millionaire California banker, the clown who let a sparrow fly out of his cap as a player in Brooklyn's Ebbetts Field, the incredibly successful manager of the New York Yankees and the entertaining loser as manager of the Mets.

"Casey Stengel has two faces," wrote Edward Linn (1973):

There is the face the public has come to know and laugh at, the gimpy, dog-eared old man winking, grimacing and babbling on in what is taken, on faith, to be profound — if not always decipherable — wisdom. The public Stengel is no myth. He is a wonderfully funny and engaging man — a wit and a comic both...But beneath the public face is the face the underlings have come to know and resent. Casey is a strong leader, the kind of leader who not only has to run the entire show but has to know that everyone else knows he's running it. (p. 67)

In other words, Casey adopted one behavior style while dealing with the public through the media and another while dealing with players and coaches in the clubhouse and on the field.

You Don't Need a Couch

Coaches don't have the leisure to observe an athlete's behavior over a lifetime. They need to know quickly how to motivate, how to discipline and how to reward. They need to know when it's safe to dress down an athlete before a crowd and when to administer reproof in private.

Coaches who want to know these things don't have to send all of their players to psychiatrists' couches or put them under sodium pentothal. Behavioral scientists have developed a number of systems for determining behavior styles. These were devised primarily for use in the corporate environment. But in working with coaches and athletes, using one such system, this author made an interesting discovery: It worked in sports as well as in business.

Among the instruments that have been used in business and industry is the Personal Profile System, copyrighted by Performax Systems International, Inc. It's the one I have used in working with athletic departments, and it is based on long-accepted behavioral concepts.

The Personal Profile System began as an effort to help dentists make friends with their patients. The assumption was that the best dentists in the world would have problems developing their practices if they didn't learn to make patients comfortable, allay their fears and win their confidence.

Back in the 1950s, the people who ran the dental school at the University of Minnesota knew they were turning out dentists who were good at taking care of teeth. However, they weren't sure they were turning out dentists who were good at taking care of people. So they sought help from Dr. John Geier, a behavioral psychologist with the university.

Dr. Geier was already developing a system for identifying behavior styles. He went to work with the dental school and came up with the Personal Profile System.

Dr. Geier relied to a great extent on information from a book by Dr. William Marsten, who helped develop the lie-detector test. Marsten's book, written in the early 1930s, was entitled *The Emotions of Normal People*. Building on that information, Dr. Geier developed his system, and it became the property of Performax.

What applies to dentists can apply to corporate presidents and to athletic coaches: You may have all the technical knowledge you need to do your job, but to be fully successful, you need to know about people too.

THE FOUR BASIC STYLES

The Personal Profile System identifies four basic behavior styles in humans. That's nothing new. About 2,400 years ago, Hippocrates identified four "humors." He believed our temperaments were controlled by blood, phlegm, black bile and yellow bile. In the 1920s, the renowned Dr. Carl Jung published a book that also divided us into four categories according to how we perceive the world. His categories were intuitors, thinkers, feelers and sensors.

For the sake of convenience, we will deal with the styles

as they are designated by The Performax system. It identifies them by four letters: D, I, S and C.

Think of D as standing for the dominating type. People who follow this style are the impatient go-getters — people of action who are more comfortable when directing others than when taking directions themselves. Vince Lombardi's axiom, "Winning isn't everything, it's the only thing," exemplifies this behavior style.

The letter I may stand for influencing or for interacting. People who follow this style like to socialize and often are theatrical. They like to do things that win applause. They add excitement to their environments, but they may engage in more horseplay than a coach likes to put up with. Olympic gymnast Mary Lou Retton's I characteristics both appealed to and challenged Bela Karolyi. Muhammad Ali and Magic Johnson also exhibit I characteristics.

The S is for steadiness. S people shun the limelight, prefer stable environments and try to avoid conflict with others. They take pride in their work and try to do it right. Henry Aaron's untheatrical but highly productive career provides an example of steadiness in sports. Otto Graham's easy-going approach to the Redskins exemplifies the steadiness factor. Tony Gwynn, three-time National League batting champion, tennis star Martina Navratilova and basketball superstar Michael Jordan are other examples.

Think of C as standing for "cautiousness," or "compliance" or perhaps "cerebral." C people are thinkers. That doesn't mean they're more intelligent than people who follow other behavior styles. It means, rather, that they trust their logic more than their hunches. They may cautiously hesitate to act until they are sure they have all the facts. They strive for compliance with their own high standards and are forever reaching for perfection. Diana Nyad, the long-distance swimmer, was a perfectionist in the water. Nadia Comaneci exhibited C characteristics as a gymnast, and so did Ted Williams as a baseball hitter.

These are the basic styles. All of us embody all four styles, but under normal circumstances, one style will be dominant.

HOW CAN WE TELL?

How can we tell which style predominates in you, in each of your staffers and in each of your players? We can tell by having players and coaches respond to a form on which they are asked to pick the adjectives that most describe them and those that least describe them. From this exercise, we can identify the Ds, the Is, the Ss and the Cs. It's fun to go through the exercise together, and once we have identified each person's dominant style, there are lots of "uh-huhs" and noddings of heads.

Soon all the players get into the spirit, and they learn to look at teammates and coaches in a new way. They'll say, "Oh, he's always got to do it his way; he's a C, you know," or "Look at Dorothy go! You can tell she's a High D."

Classical Patterns

Once we have identified the basic styles, we can go even deeper and identify a number of classical behavior patterns. These patterns vary within each basic style because each of us embodies all four behavior styles to varying degrees, and one style may play a greater or lesser role under varying conditions. A player may be an I person under normal circumstances, but become a D when the pressure is on.

The classical behavior patterns help us to understand how a player or staffer will respond under normal conditions and under pressure. Performax gives these patterns descriptive names, such as achiever, agent, appraiser, counselor, creative, developer, inspirational, investigator, objective thinker, perfectionist, persuader, practitioner, promoter, result-oriented and specialist.

The University of Illinois volleyball player who wanted coach Mike Hebert to deliver a pep talk at time-out was an I person who followed the counselor pattern. Her behavior style is predominantly I, but she scored relatively high in the S column.

The one who wanted a lesson on technique was an S person who followed the perfectionist pattern. The perfectionist is someone who scores relatively high in the C and S columns.

When conducting a workshop for an athletic department, I first plot the behavior patterns of all the players and coaches. Then, on another day, they are given a lecture about what to expect from individuals with particular patterns. Later, there is another meeting with the coaches and the team. Each person is given a packet containing a description of the behavior style of every person on the staff and team. Everybody now knows who's a D, who's an I, who's an S and who's a C.

It's always an interesting experience. The behavior patterns identified in this exercise usually conform to what the coaches and players have observed in each other. Now they know why the players and staff respond the way they do.

FROM GYM TO OFFICE

Remember how Billy Martin, Howard Cosell, Casey Stengel and John McEnroe became "different" people in different environments? Coaches need to consider whether their own behavior styles change when going from the staff meeting to the gym. So after learning the coaching staff's behavior patterns in the team setting, this author administers the profile again, asking staffers to think about themselves in a staff setting.

The results can be revealing. Laura Golden, the former women's head basketball coach at Illinois, found that she was a steady S person when working with the staff, but an interacting I when working with her team. Staffers may also follow a different pattern when working with administrators.

Coaches who know their own behavior styles are in a much better position to build effective staffs. When hiring new staffers, they can choose people with behavior styles that complement the styles of existing staffers. In assigning responsibilities to existing staff, they can play to the strengths of the individuals who work under them.

In dealing with players, they will be able to know what forms of communication are most effective with each individual on the team. They will know what motivates each player, what turns some players off and what causes some to want to give up and quit the team. They will be in a better position to judge when and under what circumstances to criticize, to reprove and to discipline.

They can choose the personal approaches that will make each player want to compete and to win.

D. DOMINANCE

- High ego strength
- Desire change
- Need direct answers
- Fear being taken advantage of
- Impatient
- Risk takers
- Not easily discouraged

I. INFLUENCING

- Emotional
- People oriented
- Need Social Recognition
- Fear loss of social approval
- Disorganized
- Memory for color
- High verbal skills

S. STEADINESS

- Best listeners
- Results orientated
- Need procedures
- Fear loss of security
- Possessive
- Quiet, but witty
- Keeps emotions hidden

C. COMPLIANCE

- Accurate
- Diplomatic
- Needs to do things right way
- Fear criticism about their work
- Can be too critical
- Seeks "Ideal" mate
- Like charts, graphs, figures

2

"D" is for Dominance

He disliked rules, objected to authority and most of his adult life did what he damned well wanted to. Yet, when he had to, he could discipline himself, and he had a continuing sense of responsibility to certain people and certain things, among them his own position as hero. (pp.11-12)

...[D]emanding, hard-driving...spiteful, vindictive...a fierce competitor with an insatiable desire to win...likes to be in control at all times. He takes command of every meeting, usually doing most of the talking.... (pp. 193, 224)

He's large and commanding, authoritative and definite and physically powerful. You believe that if he had to impose his will by force, he could do it ...There's also an incipient air of impatience, or even derision, which already insists that there's no time for trivialities. (p. 12)

I've always managed aggressively and they like that. And they like the fact that I have told my bosses what they can do with their jobs; I have stood up to my bosses. (p. 12)

He had convinced millions of Americans that his ominous, growling requests for 110 percent had been met in full and that enemy lines parted like the Red Sea when his players smelled the goal line.... (p. 21) He expected to win every game, but he did not expect much help from his players. They would have to be pushed, driven and whipped until they became extensions of [his] own will, his own grim egotistic expectation of victory. (p. 84)

The people described here are, respectively, Babe Ruth (Creamer, 1974), George Steinbrenner (Martin, 1987), Bobby Knight (Mellen, 1989), Billy Martin (1987) and Vince Lombardi (Dowling, 1970). Each passage describes a person whose behavior style is dominance. They represent 10% to 15% of the general population.

D people frequently become leaders — chief executive officers of corporations, military officers, head coaches. As athletes or coaching subordinates, they can be trouble for the coach who doesn't know how to deal with them. But properly motivated, they can be the dynamos that power an operation.

D persons are notable for their egos. Babe Ruth once was reminded that under his new contract he would make more money than President Hoover.

"I had a better year," said the Babe.

The Sultan of Swat wasn't trying to put down the president of the United States. He was just acknowledging the fact that the Babe was good. D people are that way. You say, "That was a terrific game you played tonight, Dawn," and she replies, "I know." Dawn isn't a snob; she's a D person who is acting in harmony with her behavior style.

D persons have other traits that spring from their strong egos. They have a fear of losing. Therefore, they're driven to win, and they may be inconsiderate of anyone who gets in their way.

REGGIE STIRS THE DRINK

When Reggie Jackson was first signed by the Yankees, he saw it as a chance to make a name for himself in the Big Apple. As a D person, he needed to be the superstar; there was room for no other.

But the Yankees already had a star and natural team leader — catcher Thurmon Munson, who was more low-key than Reggie. Munson had led the Yankees to the pennant in 1976 and had won the league's Most Valuable Player award. If Jackson was to become Numero Uno, Munson had to be pushed aside.

Jackson's ego was up to the task, and he wasn't about to let consideration for a likeable teammate's feelings stand in the way of his triumph. Jackson boasted about what he would do for the Yankees, then threw in this dig at Munson: "I'm the straw that stirs the drink. Munson thinks he can stir it, but he can only stir it bad" (Jackson, 1984, p. 212).

The remark shocked owner George Steinbrenner, angered manager Billy Martin, threw the Yankee clubhouse into dissension and poisoned Jackson's relationship with a man who might have been his friend. But Jackson was driven by the desire to win and the fear of losing. What's more, he went out and did what he said he was going to do. He had a brilliant record with the Yankees before riding into the sunset to play out his career in California.

Jackson was not a team player. It would be hard to imagine a Joe DiMaggio, a Henry Aaron or a Willie Stargell making that kind of statement about a teammate. But D persons don't stand out as team players. They stand out as individual performers, and the wise coach learns to capitalize on their passion to excel. Jackson's exploits as "Mr. October" added luster to his individual crown, but it also helped the Yankees win. To Jackson, the three consecutive home runs he hit in the 1978 World Series validated his self-exaltation at Munson's expense. He may have done it more for himself than for the team, but his teammates shared in the World Series money.

HOW TO DEAL WITH Ds

This kind of "move over, I'm taking charge" attitude may win games, but may also discourage talented but less aggressive players from competing, especially in scholastic and other amateur sports. It can even cause enough resentment to make players try to get even during games. It's a tendency coaches have to keep in mind when dealing with D types.

Give Them Straight Talk

In addition to their fear of losing, D persons also are afraid of being taken advantage of. The skillful coach won't try to manipulate them through subtle stratagems. D persons want no nonsense. They need to be told directly what to do, and when they ask questions, they need direct answers.

What if you don't know the straight answer to the D player's question, or you aren't ready to make a commitment? Just say you don't know, or you're not ready to commit. Dr. Eric Walker, president of Penn State, gave the model answer when Assistant Coach Joe Paterno showed up at his office to ask about his future prospects. Paterno had a job offer in hand as head coach at Yale. Before he turned it down, he wanted to be sure the head coach's job at Penn State would be his when Coach Rip Engle retired. Dr. Walker didn't hem and haw.

"If you're good enough, you'll get the job," he said. "That's the only thing that's going to count."

That was all the assurance Paterno needed.

"There was no doubt in my mind that over the years I had been good enough," he wrote (Paterno, 1989, p. 91).

Let Them Be "In Charge"

Although D persons would prefer to be in charge themselves, they will respond to strong management direction. But the manager has to recognize the D person's passion for leadership.

One way to handle the D people on your staff is to delegate responsibility to them. But watch out; given completely free rein, they may become loose cannons, charging off in directions of their own. Skillful managers give D persons their assignments, tell them what results are expected, and give them deadlines for obtaining the results. It helps also to instruct D people to report back on their progress at specified intervals.

Billy Martin's favorite owner was Bob Short of the Texas Rangers, who gave him free rein in running the team:

> We never clashed. Never argued. Not once. That's because he hired me to do a job and let me do things my

way. He let me make decisions on personnel and he never interfered. (Martin, 1987, pp. 184-85)

When Martin worked with Steinbrenner, there was at least one D person too many in Yankee Stadium.

Help Them Follow Through

D people often have good administrative and delegation skills themselves. This is fortunate because, though they are the idea people in any operation, they tend to walk away from their ideas before they have made them bear fruit.

One reason is that D people get bored with routine. They need constant challenge. A D person will undertake a project and get it going smoothly. Then, needing further challenge, the individual will undertake another project, then another and another. Soon the projects are too numerous and too demanding for one person to handle. Often Big D will become bored, put them aside and "reorder priorities," or the projects may be delegated to a subordinate. Ds are good at long-range planning, but they need others to follow through for them.

Ds are also, however, the people you turn to in an emergency. They are cool and competent, and they thrive on challenge. The D person will take charge and lead the way out.

Skip the Details

D persons use their left brains more than their right. They use deductive reasoning: from generalities to specifics. They like to think in straight lines, with no philosophical detours. They don't want to be bothered by a lot of petty details they consider to be extraneous.

When you're teaching them to drive a car, don't bother them with explanations about how the electronic ignition works, how the power is transferred from piston to crankshaft through torque converter to the drive axle. Just tell them how to start the engine, how to go forward or backward, how to keep the car in the lane and how to stop. Especially how to stop.

In football, you show them where the goal line is and tell them what route you want them to take to get across it. Don't bother them with the whys. Just tell them when, where and how.

In baseball, you tell them when to bunt and when to swing away; no need to bother them with subtleties of strategy.

D persons have trouble making up their minds when they have a lot of details to analyze before deciding among options. You can do them a favor by giving them a brief, factual analysis of each option. Then they can make the decision and run with it.

Expect Them to Tune People Out

Aversion to petty details also translates into impatience with small talk. D persons don't dawdle around water coolers or coffee pots. When others in the office are engaged in petty gossip, they tune them out.

Such minor interactions may enable the I person to pick up valuable information and insights into others' feelings and motivations. D persons aren't interested. They therefore tend to be blind to the feelings of others.

It isn't that they are deliberately uncaring. If you take the time and put forth the effort to look deep into the D person, you may be pleasantly surprised. Billy Martin found Charlie Dressen — who followed the D style — to be a genuinely nice person once he got to know him. Dressen was the kind of fellow who liked to cook up a batch of chili and crab legs in the clubhouse and invite the team to partake. Bobby Knight, the head basketball coach at the University of Indiana, established a trust fund for Landon Turner, a star player who was crippled for life in an automobile in the summer of '81. But it wasn't the kind of thing Knight went around bragging about. And those who knew Vince Lombardi well could see in him a generosity and sense of caring that the great coach was reluctant to acknowledge.

Of Mike Ditka, player Jim Osborne observed: "First couple of weeks I was thinking, 'Here we go again. This guy is gonna kill us.' But Mike, he's the kind of man if you've got a problem at three in the morning, he's the guy to call" (Stamborski, 1988, pp. 173-74).

Most D persons just don't understand how their words and deeds have impact on others. Knight is frequently given to imputing canine ancestry to everyone from opposing players to basketball goalposts that refuse to accept the balls into their baskets.

"In my language, son of a bitch is a pronoun," he once said. Like most D persons, Knight doesn't like to appear soft, and he often masks tender feelings by needling people. Wrote author Joan Mellen (1989):

> The needling both expresses and wards off intimacy. It's an affectionate way he has of distancing himself from people, rather like a magnetic screen that comes up and down at will. (p. 13)

Know Once is Enough

D people don't believe in repetition. Once you've explained something to them, they don't want to hear it again. And D persons don't like to repeat themselves.

The person who wants a spouse who daily says "I love you" and in other ways provides constant assurance of affection and devotion shouldn't marry a D person. As far as the D person is concerned, the "I do" at the altar says it all. The spouse is expected to take that as assurance enough that the love and support are there.

The D person who is a coach should remember, though, that a one-time statement of approval may provide little or no motivation for a team or player, especially if there are a lot of Is and Ss in the line-up. And often it is necessary to reinforce information in young minds by repeating it constantly.

Count Fact Over Feelings

D persons are not averse to compliments. They enjoy being told they're good. But remember, a D person doesn't like to appear soft.

On the volleyball court, Denise, a D person, noticed that Salley was having trouble with her serve. She watched Salley for a while in practice, then went over to her.

"I think I can help you sharpen up that serve if you'd like to spend a little time with me after practice."

Salley took her up on it, and after a couple of hours of practice, Denise had her serving like a pro.

The gesture wasn't lost on Coach Simpson.

"That was really sweet of you to take the time to help Salley," he said. "It shows you've got the team's interests at heart and it also shows what a caring person you are. I'm proud of you."

Denise shuffled her feet in embarrassment.

"I just didn't want us blowing a game because of her wacky serves," she said.

Assistant Coach Inman had also noticed what Denise did, but she recognized Denise as a D person.

She approached her later and said, "Hey, thanks for helping Salley with her serve. I hadn't quite figured out what she was doing wrong, but you picked up on the problem right away. That's gonna help us put some more points on the board, and we can chalk them up to you."

Denise beamed. "Glad to be of help," she said.

What was the difference between the two approaches?

Coach Simpson approached Denise on the basis of feelings; Coach Inman approached her on the basis of facts and results. It didn't raise Denise's morale at all to be told that she was a sweet, caring person. What helped was the recognition that she had gotten results where someone else had failed.

Remember Denise when dealing with D-type athletes. When your star basketball player is a D person, don't tell her what a wonderful person she is. Tell her how great she performs at the free-throw line or what a marvelous hook shot she has. Keep the comments focused on performance, not on personality.

COUNSELING Ds

The same principles apply when you're counseling D persons. Focus on tasks more than on feelings.

Dale was an outfielder for the Midville Pirates. For several games his fielding had not been up to par. It wasn't a question of dropped balls or bad throws. Dale just wasn't making the extra effort to go after the close ones.

After one game in which a looping fly fell in front of Dale for a game-winning single, Coach Dawson called him aside.

"What's the matter Dale? You haven't been hustling these last few games. You could have had that ball if you'd been on your toes, and it cost us the game. What's on your mind, fellow? Your morale doesn't seem to be up to normal. I want to see you go out there and play some heads-up baseball."

Dale's response was angry and defensive.

"That wasn't the only hit they got all day, you know, Coach. I didn't let in the other four runs. And besides, I got three put-outs and I didn't make one error. Why are you putting me down just because I played the guy deep and he dropped one in front of me? Why don't you ask the second baseman why he didn't get it?"

Later, Assistant Coach Sanders talked to Dale.

"Don't be too hard on Coach Dawson," he said. "He's like you; he doesn't like to lose. I know that you're the best outfielder on the team. If anybody can play that position, you can.

"But I've noticed several close ones recently that ordinarily you would have snagged. For some reason or other, you're not getting your normal jump on the ball. How about taking a look at how you're playing the position and getting back to me Thursday. I'd like to know how you think you can improve your performance. You got three put-outs today, and that's fine. If you can make four or five a game, it'll take a lot of pressure off the pitcher and off our other batters."

Dale promised Coach Sanders he'd lick his problem.

The difference between the two approaches was Sanders' emphasis on results instead of feelings and his involvement of Dale in the solution.

As a D person, Dale thrives on challenge. Coach Sanders gave him a challenge: Increase the number of put-outs per game. Sanders didn't talk about vague terms, such as morale and hustle. He talked about performance: The close ones were dropping in for hits. He demonstrated the difference between what Dale was doing and what he would like for him to do. He asked Dale to find a solution to the problem, and he gave him a definite time frame for finding it.

Remember those guidelines when counseling or correcting a D person: Stick to facts, not feelings. Point out the gap between present performance and desired performance. Ask the person being counseled to look for a solution, and establish a time frame. And be willing to listen to the D person's suggestions.

THE ANGRY OUTBURST FACTOR

D persons are extroverts, which means they don't ventilate pressure inwardly. When John McEnroe is on the wrong end of a bad call, he never ponders whether he might be wrong and the official right. He doesn't shrug it off with a philosophical "Everybody makes mistakes." He doesn't reason that the close calls balance out; you win some, you lose some. When the call goes against him, he gets angry and he lets his anger out. That's D-person behavior.

But off the court, in the privacy of a bar, away from the pressure to win, McEnroe has been known to go to unusual lengths to avoid confrontation with unruly types. When D persons go into a rage, it's usually just to release pressure. They rarely follow through with violent actions (although Billy Martin occasionally did).

"Nobody liked hassles less than I do," asserts Coach Knight. "I'd just like to go through life without another hassle. But it will be unavoidable because I'll take certain stands on things and somebody will make some comment, and I'll say, 'That's an idiotic thing to say,' because it is idiotic to say" (Mellon, 1989, p. 59). There's no pretense with D persons.

THE D AS A COACH

If your coaching style is D, you may want to think a bit about how others are perceiving you.

As a strong-willed person, you are self-motivated. You don't need the daily laying on of hands to get you into the winning spirit. You are impatient, and you want everyone else to share your impatience — to get on the stick, NOW! You stay after hours and work into the night because you have that insatiable drive to win.

Your example may be helpful in setting a high standard for others to follow. But your methods may be exhausting to other behavior types. They may need your understanding more than they need your prodding. Your criticism may destroy their morale instead of goading them to greater performance. They may respond more readily to praise. If you're a D coach, look for something your staff and your players are doing right, and praise them for it.

Penn State's Joe Paterno learned early in his career to curb his impatience with others' pace of learning:

> I'd look at a kid and see that when he was going to throw he had a habit of holding the ball lower than when he was going to hand it off or run, or his footwork was bad, or this or that was bad. He might make five or six kinds of mistakes and I wanted him to fix them all in one day. (Paterno, 1989, p. 83)

But Paterno learned patience from the coaches he had worked with at Brown, including Rip Engle, the one he followed from Brown to Penn State:

> Spend a couple of days with a kid on his footwork and get it right. Then go to the next part and get that right. They taught me to analyze a problem, put down a specific plan for how to get from here to there, step by step, in the time we had available. (Paterno, 1989, p. 83)

The D side of Paterno's behavior was learning from a coach with S characteristics.

Players Aren't Pawns

D coaches may regard their players as so many pawns.

Irving hated playing catcher for the Crossville Sentinels. He found the position too confining and too passive. He longed to play the infield, where he could roam the turf, snagging grounders and nailing runners.

Coach Dodson didn't care what Irving wanted. Infielders were a dime a dozen and you could find them on any sandlot. He had decided that Irving would make the best catcher of all the boys who went out for baseball. So he told him, "You play behind the plate or you don't play at all."

Irving played, and he performed competently. But he had a mediocre season at the plate. The next year he went out for the basketball team and forgot all about baseball.

Dodson lost a potentially valuable player because his zeal to win caused him to overlook the desires of the individual. While no coach can allow the players to run the team, every coach should learn to listen creatively to the desires and aspirations of individual players. In industry, in academe and on the playing field, there's a truism: We're more productive when we're doing something that makes us happy. Playing behind the plate didn't make Irving happy.

Evaluating the Lombardi Approach

Vince Lombardi was a D person who believed strongly that tactics, not people, won football games.

At Green Bay, he built his team around that principle. When Bart Starr threw to a receiver, he didn't make the choice on the basis of the receiver's great hands or his ability to get beyond the secondary. Lombardi taught Starr to read the opposing defense, pick out the weak spots and throw to them, regardless of which receiver happened to be in the spot. Starr was not throwing to individuals; he was throwing to the Xs on his play charts.

When Lombardi moved to Washington, he inherited quarterback Sonny Jurgensen, reputed to have the most accurate arm in the National Football League. Jurgensen had two fine receivers in Charlie Taylor and Sonny Smith. He knew when to rely on Taylor's strong legs and when to opt for Smith's good hands. When Jurgensen started a play, he knew to whom he wanted to throw and that primary receiver was the first person for whom he'd look.

But that wasn't Lombardi's style. He did not believe in relying on individual talents. He believed in following a system that would work regardless of the talents involved.

As Tom Dowling (1970) wrote:

> For Lombardi, a team was not eleven individuals, some of them more dependable than others. It was one unit with 11 parts, and when one part ceased to function, the whole unit broke down; the chances of that breakdown were reduced when the responsibilities of each player were kept simple but interconnected. (p. 85)

Given time, Lombardi might have molded the Redskins into the type of winning machine that he had produced in Green Bay. As it happened, time was short for the great coach. His stay with the Redskins, again quoting Dowling (1970), was "six months of conflict, pressure, insecurity and fear" (p. 6).

Lombardi followed the D person's tendency to regard players as pawns. Mike Ditka acknowledged that he is sometimes perceived as having the same attitude.

"Sometimes players feel I don't think they're important to the team," he said. "That's not true." But on another occasion, he remarked, "My players play hard because I think they know they have to play hard to stay on the field. There's nobody I wouldn't replace" (Stamborski, 1988, p. 132-33).

That's the D person talking.

In professional sports, such relentless, hard-driving methods can succeed, given a D-type coach with enough time, energy and force of character. In scholastic sports, the D's drive to win must be tempered by compassion, by the goal of developing people as well as teams and by the reluctance of administration and parents to tolerate ruthless tactics.

Ditka was speaking as a D coach when he said, "...I want to win. That's the only thing I want to do. If a player wants to win, he should have no problem. If he wants to be patted on the butt every time he does something wrong, then he'll have a problem."

Ditka is no coddler of players. But D coaches in pro football can follow their win-at-all-costs instincts further than prudence allows a scholastic coach to go.

To a pro athlete, Vince Lombardi could repeat his father's maxim: "Hurt is in the mind." He could say to Bob Long, suffering from a torn cartilage in the knee, "Get up, run on that leg, there's no pain in that leg." He could put Long back into uniform after doctors had advised him to be out for the season, send him into a tough pass pattern and, when the leg gave out again, shout, "Get up! Run on that leg! There's nothing left in that...leg to hurt!" (Dowling, 1970, p. 55).

The scholastic coach who did that would be in deep trouble with parents and administrators. Even in professional sports, this intense drive to win can blind the coach to long-range consequences. Vince Promuto played for Lombardi when he had a bad case of water on the knee. His performance helped the team in that game, but Promuto says it set his recovery back a month (Dowling, 1970, p. 56).

HOW TO HARNESS Ds

D persons are seldom happy with their environment. They look for ways to change it, and they're impatient for the change.

The D coach needs to understand that not all people are as ready for change. The world is made up of progressive spirits eager to carve out a new tomorrow and guardians of tradition eager to preserve the treasures of the past. In politics they're known as liberals and conservatives. The world needs both.

The wise D person will listen to defenders of the status quo. Perhaps change is desirable, but before clearing the forest it might be helpful to identify a few tall redwoods worth sparing.

Confront Them

Suppose you're an I, S or C and you have to deal with a D person. You may feel that stopping one is like trying to stop Herschel Walker with a bunch of junior-varsity lightweights.

Well, you don't stop them by throwing hints or by trying to manipulate them. They'll resent you for it. You have to confront them directly.

This can be difficult because D persons can be intimidating. The story is told about Miller Huggins, the diminutive Yankee manager, who once vowed to nip in the bud the flagrant carousing of one George Herman Ruth.

"I'm gonna have a talk with the Babe," Huggins told a press conference.

Shortly afterwards, a writer informed Huggins that Ruth was coming down the hall, smoking a black cigar and acting his usual arrogant self.

"Ok, I'm gonna talk to him," said Huggins.

And he did. He confronted the big slugger, looked him straight in the eye, and said, "Hiya, Babe" (Thorn, 1976, pp. 51-52).

The Babe never reformed throughout his career.

The truth is, D persons respect those who stand up to them, although they may not be pleased about it at the time. Still, direct confrontation is better than beating around the bush.

Help Them Win

Another way to deal with D people is to help them win. This "winning" doesn't necessarily have to be on the playing field. It can mean succeeding in what they do. If D people are overcommitted — as they frequently are — you can pitch in and help them get their work done. You may be able to show them how to organize their work more efficiently, or suggest ways they can delegate. Remember: D persons may lunge for victory to feed their own egos. But if they're on your side, they'll take you right into the winner's circle with them.

D persons are natural risk-takers. They'll plunge into things that would scare other people, and they won't even think they're taking risks.

It's fourth and one on your own 30, and you're a field goal down with enough time for one more possession before the final gun.

"Punt," says the cautious C. "Go for the bomb," says the risk-taking D.

If you're a cautious baseball manager, you don't want a D person for a third-base coach.

D persons wouldn't admit it, but fear is what drives many of them to succeed. They're afraid of exposure and rejection. Beneath their bravado is a fear of inadequacy. Deep down, they're afraid that if they lose, they won't be loved or accepted. Because they have a yearning to control, they're afraid that if they lose, people will no longer follow them.

If you're coaching youngsters, it's worthwhile to assure D players that your esteem for them doesn't depend upon constant winning—that one's performance as an athlete is something quite distinct from one's value as a person.

Be Aware of Strengths and Weaknesses

D-type persons can be valuable as players, coaches and staffers.

We have to play to their strengths: They are full of confidence. They are a fountain of ideas. They have an intense drive to lead and to win. They are take-charge people. They thrive on challenge. They are persistent. They make quick decisions and get immediate results. They are good long-range planners and good problem solvers. We have to compensate for their weaknesses: They are insensitive to others. They are impatient. They disregard risks. They are inflexible and unyielding. They take on too much and demand too much of others. They are inattentive to detail.

We can help them contribute by providing them with new challenges and difficult assignments.

Are all their egos worth tolerating?

Remember, the Yankees are still playing in "The House That Ruth Built."

D. DOMINANCE

- High ego strength
- Desire change
- Need direct answers
- Fear being taken advantage of
- Impatient
- Risk takers
- Not easily discouraged

I. INFLUENCING

- Emotional
- People oriented
- Need Social Recognition
- Fear loss of social approval
- Disorganized
- Memory for color
- High verbal skills

S. STEADINESS

- Best listeners
- Results orientated
- Need procedures
- Fear loss of security
- Possessive
- Quiet, but witty
- Keeps emotions hidden

C. COMPLIANCE

- Accurate
- Diplomatic
- Needs to do things right way
- Fear criticism about their work
- Can be too critical
- Seeks "ideal" mate
- Like charts, graphs, figures

3

"I" is for Interaction

Probably the most famous home run in history was struck on Oct. 1, 1932, in the fifth inning of a World Series game between the New York Yankees and the Chicago Cubs.

The game was tied 4-4. The pitcher was Charlie Root. The batter was Babe Ruth. Babe took two strikes from Root, calling each pitch even before the umpire did. Babe watched as Root wasted two pitches. Then Ruth pointed to the flagpole in center field. He proceeded to belt the next pitch into the stands, just a few feet to one side of the flagpole. The awesome Bambino was his usual intimidating self at the plate.

But the Babe's gesture was not original, nor can it compare in theatrical flare with the antics of one Herman "Germany" Schaefer, who played second base for the Detroit Tigers in the early part of the 20th century.

LADEEZ AND GENTLEMEN

In a game against the White Sox, Schaefer was taking a terrible razzing from the fans. His first two times at bat, the Sox got him out.

On his third appearance, Schaefer raised his hands for silence.

"Ladeez and gentlemen!" he intoned. "Pay close attention. You are about to witness a marvelous exhibition of the art of batting by the one — the only — the world's greatest hitter — Germany Schaefer!"

The first pitch was a strike. Schaefer bowed: "That's one for the build-up." The second pitch also was a strike. Schaefer tipped his cap: "That's just for suspense!" On the third throw, the batter knocked the ball into the left field stands for a home run.

As he touched first, Schaefer turned to the stands and yelled, "Schaefer beats it out to first!" At second, he threw a hook slide, got up and shouted, "Schaefer gets to second before the ball!" Then he raced to third, shouting, "Schaefer safe by a mile." He slid into home, raising a cloud of dust. Then he brushed himself off, turned to the crowd, and announced, "This concludes the great batting exhibition for this afternoon. Mr. Herman Schaefer, the world's greatest hitter, thanks you each and every one for your kind attention" (Thorn, 1976, p. 51-52).

The Babe's act was the ego-driven accomplishment of a dominant personality. Germany Schaefer was acting in the mold of an influencing interactor — the I person among our profiles.

THE CHILD IN US ALL

D and I persons are all extroverts, but there's a more playful quality to the I. To paraphrase Roy Campanella, the great Dodger catcher, to be a successful athlete, you've got to be an adult. But you've got to have a lot of child in you too. The child is more visible in the I.

We see the child in Pete Rose, sprinting to first base after a walk, sliding head first into third on a hit-and-run play, chattering with infielders, umpires and even opposing players when he's in the field or on base. We see the child in Muhammad Ali, skipping around the ring after a knockout as if he'd just won the lollipop in a playground pitch-and-toss competition.

We see the child in Mae Faggs, the Olympic runner from Tennessee State, prancing up to the starting line, getting into position, looking down the line, and saying, "I'm gonna be first—who's gonna be second?" (Temple, 1980, p. 20).

When Vince Lombardi asked Paul Hornung whether he wanted to be a playboy or a professional football player,

Hornung answered, "Both." And Hornung was, combining child and adult in one personality.

I persons are driven by a need for recognition. These are the people who want to be liked. Natural cheerleaders, they are optimistic, enthusiastic and personable.

They can also be entertaining. The razzing Chicago fans gave way to laughter and applause after Germany Shaefer's display of showmanship around the diamond. Before Casey Stengel's formidable five-year string of American League pennants with the Yankees, he was best known for the time he came to bat for the Dodgers, doffed his hat and let a sparrow fly out.

Willie's Flying Cap

In a less clownish way, Willie Mays was also an entertainer. The flying cap was a trademark of the Say-Hey Kid. But Mays wasn't flipping his lid by accident. The cap stayed securely on Willie's head when he first joined the Giants in 1951. That's because the Giants issued him a cap that fit.

"But after a while," wrote Willie:

> I started thinking about what I could do to give the fans a show, generate a little more excitement. So I came up with a gimmick. I started wearing a cap that was too big for me, and sure enough, every time I ran from first to second and wheeled to my left, that cap would simply fly off just as if I'd been running so fast I'd run out from under. The cap would fly off when I stole a base, and so after dusting myself off I'd have to go back and pick it up. The moment's delay would keep the fans worked up and make the opposing pitcher think a bit more about the spot I'd got him in, which was fine with me. (Mays, 1988, p. 14)

"Hello, Mary Lou"

Is are people-oriented. They like to be around people, especially when they can be the charming centers of attention. The I person never meets a stranger and always wants to be one of the gang.

Mary Lou Retton was going nowhere as a gymnast while she did her training in her hometown of Fairmount, West

Virginia. There were no other competitive gymnasts in town, so when she traveled to compete, she went alone instead of as part of a team. She recalls:

> I had no teammates from my own club to hang out with, and it was kind of sad and boring. I'd be in a hotel room all by myself, and I'd hear girls from some other club yelling and having fun next door. Then, when I went into competition, I'd be by myself in a group. I really felt lonely.

Mary Lou came into her own when she went to train at Bela Karolyi's gym in Houston. There, she not only found other gymnasts with whom she could interact, but also competitors toward whom she could look and say, "Gosh, I've got to do better than she" (Retton and Karolyi, 1986, p. 19).

Magic in the Bahamas

Pat Riley (1988), coach of the Los Angeles Lakers, was able to spot an I person at a distance along a beach in the Bahamas during an off-season visit with one of his players, Mychal Thompson. He wrote:

> I looked down the beach. There was a figure walking in our direction, maybe 800 yards away. I took off my glasses and squinted. This was a big guy. But most of the Bahamian men are tall; it could have been anybody. This guy ran out into the surf to shake somebody's hand. Then he walked up the sand to slap five with somebody else and do a little pirouette. He kept walking our way until I could see that he was wearing a big, loose, gray T-shirt and a little red bikini bathing suit.

It was Riley's wife, Chris, who put a name to the image: "That's Magic." It was Earvin "Magic" Johnson, whom Riley describes as "the center of fun at every party and an amazing unstoppable force in every game" (p. 3-4).

The Lovable Lasorda

Billy Martin (1987) found Tommy Lasorda's chummy approach to managing foreign to Martin's instincts, though he acknowledged that they worked for the Dodger manager.

"Tommy's strength as a manager seems to be as a motivator, a positive thinker," wrote Billy. "But all that hugging and everything with his players, I don't believe in it" (p. 33).

Though their methods were as different as the behavior styles of a D and an I, Martin and Lasorda were both successful major league baseball managers.

The I's natural gregariousness may hide an inner pain. The I person needs the applause to soothe the pain. When the applause dies, the hurt returns. Ergo, the constant quest for applause. When you find yourself getting frustrated with the team show-off, try to get to know the individual a little better. The showboating may hide a hurt.

OFFENSIVE GLORY

On the athletic court or field, the I person generally prefers the offensive position. The fans cheer the touchdown more than the tackle, the home run more than the double play. I persons make good runners in football and good finishers in soccer. They relish the glory of the moment, the opportunity to earn the applause.

"I don't know why Paul was the type of pressure player he was," admitted Vince Lombardi, the quintessential D person, in discussing Paul Hornung's exploits. "Maybe it was because he knew the tougher the situation, the more glory there was for him in it" (Dowling, 1970, p. 316).

Ed Temple (1980) made a similar comment about Barbara Jones, captain of the 400-meter relay team that set a new world and Olympic record in Rome:

> B.J. was always what you would call a money runner. If we'd go to a small meet, she wouldn't exert herself too much. But if you got her in front of cheering crowds, she'd make the rest of the runners blow a gasket. (p. 67)

I persons will be daring and experimental in team play, often developing unusual moves and testing them out in game situations. Their "I can do it" attitude often leads them to oversell themselves. They think they already know how to make a double play, kick a field goal, serve a volleyball or sink a basket from the top of the key. The coach's task is to curb their overconfidence without destroying their initiative.

The Budding Rose

That's what concerned Phil Seghi, the man who signed Pete Rose for the Cincinnati Reds. Pete signed his contract after graduating from high school, which meant the minor-league season was well under way. Ineligible to play high-school baseball that year, Pete had played two or three times a week with an amateur league in Dayton, Ohio.

Seghi gave Rose a choice: He could wait until spring and go to the tryouts in Tampa, or he could report immediately to the Reds' Geneva, New York, farm club. Seghi told him:

> I'll be honest with you, Pete. I know you've been playing ball a couple of times a week, but you're going to have to face facts. You're not really in shape to play....But if you really want to go to Geneva, fine. We don't care if you go up there and hit .100. What we really care about is the effect it will have on you. After all, in Dayton you were tearing the league apart. It won't happen that way in Geneva because you're not ready. They'll be tearing you apart.

Pete, the rah-rah eager beaver, decided to go to Geneva, ready or not. He was a greenhorn, but he was also an I person, with a knack for relating to people:

> After the first few days, I felt I'd been there all my life...[but] two and a half months of experience that year made the big fat difference between how good they looked and how dumb I looked....My fielding was pretty good, but it wasn't sensational. My hitting, just like Mr. Seghi predicted, was way off. I was getting the blues fast. (Rose, 1970, pp. 66-67)

Rose had the talent and the hustle to overcome the blues and eventually to amass more major-league hits than even the redoubtable Ty Cobb. The I player's mentor will have to determine when it's all right to go with the athlete's confidence and when to throw in a dash of realism.

ACTION IN A HURRY

I persons are not very good at time management. Their appetite for excitement leads them to take on too many projects at once. They'll get distracted by more interesting diversions until the last moment, then rush their job to completion.

It's the I person who forgets important occasions and shows up at the last minute for practice. But if you have something that needs doing at the last moment, go to your Is. If they have to stay up all night to get the project done, they'll do it. It goes back to their poor time management. Because they're not good at organizing their time, they end up doing things at the last minute. But because they are eager for applause, they'll do them well. They know that botched jobs bring humiliation, not glory.

ROWDIEST OF THE ROWDY

Because they're looking for the group's approval, Is are easily influenced by companions. Surrounded by rowdy friends, they'll be the rowdiest.

When Pete Rose was a minor leaguer, he allowed two companions to persuade him to climb through the window of their second-floor hotel room and edge around a narrow roof ledge to check out a party in the adjoining room. On another occasion, riding in a station wagon between minor-league engagements, Pete climbed out the tailgate window while the car was cruising down the road, crawled onto the roof and sat perched atop the car for several miles. And just sitting on the rooftop and taking the wind at 60 miles per hour wasn't good enough for Pete. To really enjoy the experience, he had to have an audience. So he crawled forward, leaned over the windshield and waved to the driver. It was foolhardy, but Rose got the attention he wanted (Rose, 1970, pp. 71-72).

Unfortunately, Rose allowed his behavior to be influenced by the wrong kind of companions. His interaction with gamblers cost him his position in Cincinnati and tarnished his hard-won image.

"PAY ATTENTION TO ME"

When the I is there, you know it. At least, the I wants you to know it.

So your work day starts at 8 a.m. Big D is there at 7:30 to get the jump on everyone. The Ss and Cs are at their work stations by 7:55. Ms. I breezes in at 30 seconds before the hour.

"Hi everybody, how's it going? Great morning, huh?"

The response is tepid. It isn't that nobody notices her; it's just that the rest of the people are there to work, and that's what they're doing. Ms. I, somewhat deflated, spends the first 20 minutes at her desk trying to figure out why nobody likes her anymore.

The truth is that everyone likes her just as much today as they did at 5 p.m. yesterday. But Ms. I's instincts tell her otherwise. She's motivated by recognition from others. And nobody has recognized her presence.

If you work around I people, you can help start their days off on a motivational note. When they come in, just look at them, give them a bright smile and say, "Hi. Good to see you." Then they'll feel wanted.

The Face Tells All

When I people show up for work or practice, you'll know immediately how they feel. Their bum moods are obvious to everyone. Their great moods shine like flashing neon advertisements.

"You could always tell what I was thinking just by looking at my face," observed Mary Lou Retton. "I can't hold it in. I'd come in some days when the last thing I wanted to do was work out, and Bela would see that and start making jokes, massaging my shoulders and getting me pumped up." Bela Karolyi, on the other hand, found that Nadia Comaneci's face rarely told him what mood she was in.

"Oh, I hate the ones with the long face," Karolyi would tell Retton. "You cannot tell what they are thinking" (Retton and Karolyi, 1986, p. 79).

The Love to Talk

I persons love to talk, especially about themselves. They prefer talking to writing. If you ask Coach I to send you a memo on the status of the new uniforms, she'll probably say, "Can I get back with you by phone?"

When it comes to oral communication, the I person stands out.

Verbosity

Casey Stengel's verbosity is legendary. He was an accomplished storyteller, and he did a lot of talking on the bench. Billy Martin, one of his successors as a Yankee manager, recalled that often when he was confronting a particular situation, he would recall something that Stengel had said and would know exactly what to do.

Like most I people, Stengel had his playful side, too. Martin (1987) remembers the time he went off to the far end of the bench and sulked after Casey had benched him. Eventually, the manager walked over to his volatile problem child and said, "Whassa matter? Is widdo Biwwy mad at me? Will you take your widdo gwove and go out and pway second base?" (p. 45).

Martin characterized Lasorda as a latter-day Casey Stengel. Calling him a professional bull-shooter by nature, Martin said:

> He likes to...tell stories and jokes...He really enjoys being funny...He's trying to be a comedian and a manager at the same time, and he gets a big kick out of it. Besides, it works for him. (p. 33)

Word Play

I persons are also good at manipulating the language to achieve their objectives.

In the old days, before the spitball was outlawed, the Pittsburgh Pirates had a pitcher, Marty O'Toole, who moistened his spitter by licking the horsehide directly. Once, when O'Toole was spraying the Philadelphia Phillies with his spitball, Fred Luderus, the Phillies' first baseman, stuck a tube of liniment in his hip pocket. Every time the ball would come to him, he'd rub it with liniment. (Those were the days when a single ball might last for an entire game.) By the third inning, O'Toole's tongue was so inflamed he had to be taken out of the game. The Pirates protested loudly. But Charlie Dooin, the Phillies' manager, had his speech cleverly planned. He told the umpire:

> I ordered Luderus to do it to protect my boys. That nasty habit of O'Toole's was putting millions of germs on every pitch. Every time O'Toole spits on that ball, we're going to disinfect it. There's nothing in the rules that says we don't have the right to protect our health. (Thorn, 1976, p. 54)

Like their fellow extroverts of the D persuasion, Is are not noted for their follow-through. Their minds take in the global picture and balk at the boring details. Hence, once they get away from the grand scheme and get down to the nitty gritty, they lose interest.

THE BIG PICTURE

This aversion to detail may cause them to jump off before they know where they're going to land. I persons see the big picture and think they know all the details as well. Therefore, they may act impulsively, before they have all the facts. I persons tend to go with gut decisions, letting their intuition guide them. This may work if their intuition is guided by long experience or careful study. But if I coaches aren't careful, they can be embarrassed by going off half-cocked.

As an I person, I normally read for the big picture, taking in the narrative in clumps. But when doing serious reading, for research or information, I have to read like a C person, one word or one idea at a time. Different behavior styles have to be adopted for different circumstances. If you're an I person, keep that in mind. If you're coaching I persons, pass along the hint to them.

Remember—there is a great fear among I people: the fear of loss of social approval. Hand in hand with that fear is the dread of embarrassment.

Fear

If Babe Ruth's called shot was the most famous home run in history, the second most famous must have been Bobby Thomson's pennant-winning blast for the New York Giants in the 1951 National League play-offs. What many people don't remember is that there was a rookie outfielder in the on-deck circle praying for Thomson to get on.

Willie Mays wasn't just praying because he wanted the Giants to win the pennant. He was praying because if Thomson failed to get on, Willie would be coming to bat with two outs and the tying run on base. He could be the hero of the game, or he could make the last out of the season.

And Willie's prayer was, "Please don't let it be me. Don't let me come to bat now, God" (Mays, 1988, p. 15).

Later, when he had the confidence in his own ability, Willie Mays would be praying for the opportunity to come to bat with the tying run on base. But this time, in his rookie year, when he was 1 for 10 in the play-offs, Willie was frightened of the embarrassment that might come with a strikeout, an easy grounder or a pop fly. The I person prayed for the cup to pass.

Embarrassment

As an I person, I can tell you how it feels: Suppose I'm walking across a parking lot, briefcase in hand, and I stumble and fall. There I am, sprawled on the pavement, hose shredded, knee bleeding, papers scattered — a public spectacle.

What will I do?

I'll stuff those papers back into my briefcase, get back on my feet as quickly as possible and hurry to my car to compose myself out of the public eye.

The S person would take the time to put her papers in order, neatly replacing them in her briefcase. Then she would calmly get up, brush herself off and tend to the bleeding knee.

Is will do anything to avoid public humiliation.

Mary Lou Retton provides us with an even more dramatic example. Once an ABC television crew was filming workouts at Bela Karolyi's Houston gym. Mary Lou was doing a free hip circle on the low bar when her hands slipped. She landed on her chin and got up with a bleeding mouth. The camera was seeing it all. Mary Lou's face and actions betrayed her profound distress.

Bela Karolyi didn't realize the depth of that distress. He barked at his star pupil and ordered her to the bathroom to clean up. After a trip to the emergency room, Mary Lou went home crying. Karolyi spoke to her by telephone and berated her for acting like a baby.

It was not the tactic to use on a sensitive I. Mary Lou was ready to go home to West Virginia. Her mother cautioned her against doing anything rash, but she was packed and ready to leave. But Karolyi, realizing that he was not dealing with Comaneci the perfectionist, showed up the next day with an apologetic look on his face, and he gave her a big hug. Mary Lou went on to achieve the glory she sought (Retton and Karolyi, 1986, p. 31).

THE RIGHT TIMING

Karolyi had caught Retton in an embarrassing moment and had compounded the embarrassment by yelling at her in public. Wise coaches will avoid chewing out I persons in front of others or doing anything else that might cause them public embarrassment.

While working with the women's volleyball team at the University of Illinois, I saw another example of an I person's sensitivity to embarrassment.

A player — let's call her Inez — known by me to be an I, missed a return. A couple of plays later, Coach Mike Hebert called time out and pulled her from the line-up. She was flushed with anger and was muttering something to herself.

"It wasn't my fault," she said, when asked what was wrong. Another player had called for the ball and Inez had held back to let her return it. The other player had failed to make the play.

If that was the case, I said, she shouldn't worry about it. She had done her part.

"But they don't know it," she said, gesturing toward the crowd.

Later, I talked to Coach Hebert about it. Mike knew the

player was upset and that her anger had affected her play for the rest of the game. But he hadn't guessed why. He hadn't pulled her because she missed the ball; he had pulled her because it was time to rotate some players. But to Inez, it looked as though she was being pulled because of an error and was being put on public display for the offense.

If you're going to pull an I person from the line-up because of a bad play, try to put some distance between the offense and your reaction. Otherwise, you're delivering a devastating blow to morale.

Whatever you do, don't criticize an I person in public. If criticism is necessary, don't yell it across the gym. Take your player aside, either to a private corner of the gym or to your office. If you do your talking in public, I persons won't hear you. They'll be thinking about the audience and how it perceives them, not about anything you're saying.

THE NEED FOR ACCLAIM

I people live for acclaim. People's admiration means more to them than to any other behavior type. It isn't whether you win or lose, it's how the crowd perceives you.

Listen to Pete Rose (1970) describing his first appearance with the Cincinnati Reds. It was only a base on balls, but Charlie Hustle made it something worth applauding:

> I took off for first base like a bird. That was the first time the hometown fans had seen the way I had been hustling all my life. I didn't walk to first. I didn't stroll. I scooted as if my life depended on it. And there I stood, on first, listening to the way the fans reacted. There was one big cheer. And it was real good to hear that. (p. 98)

The smart coach knows how to use this taste for acclaim as a motivating force, even when reprimanding.

Dizzy the Great

Frankie Frisch did that admirably once when he slapped a midnight curfew on his St. Louis Cardinals during a tight pennant race. One night, the midnight hour struck and four players were still out. Among them was Dizzy Dean, his brilliant and flamboyant pitching ace. Frisch fined three of the players $200 each, but nailed Dizzy for $400.

Dizzy was hurt.

"After all," he protested, "It ain't like I was doing something different than those other three guys."

Frisch threw an arm around Dean's shoulder:

"Why, Diz, you're not the same as those other guys. You're the star of this team. You're the great Dizzy Dean. Everything about you has got to be bigger and better than anybody else. And that goes for the fines too."

That was all Dizzy's ego needed to hear.

"Danged if you ain't right," he admitted, and paid his fine.

Frisch was ingeniously accomplishing two objectives at once: He was satisfying his star pitcher's need for acclaim while punishing his negative behavior. (Thorn, 1976, p. 116)

THE WAY TO HANDLE Is

In dealing with I athletes, the successful coach will remember the factors that drive their behavior. Frequent assurances that the player doesn't have to be entertaining to be loved can be helpful. But the desire to put on a show can motivate an I person to great accomplishments.

Serious discussions can help I players put their behavior in perspective. Frequent failures can also be a valuable teacher. The I person will not persist in behavior that brings repeated embarrassment.

Remember What Motivates

When it's necessary to punish I persons, remember what turns them on: interaction with other people. Punishment can consist of denying them the opportunity to mingle with their friends. Send them off for individual drills. Or make them sit at desks and write out what they did wrong. This forces them into introspection, and a little introspection never hurt the over-exuberant extrovert.

Discerning coaches will not give their I players too much to do at once. Too many details will overwhelm them. The way to teach them is to get them involved. They like hands-on learning. If you want to teach a tricky kick to an I soccer player, by all means demonstrate. But then let the player try it. After he's tried it, get him to demonstrate that he understands what you've taught him. That allows you to give him some feedback. If you don't work with I people in this structured way, they'll jump in and try it before they've mastered it, and this will make you and them look silly.

If you have a disagreement with an I person, try not to argue. If trapped, they're masters of the art of manipulation.

Catcher Jimmy Wilson of the St. Louis Cardinals learned that lesson when he found some of his prized silk shirts missing. He later spied one of them on a rookie pitcher, a young kid from the mountains who had just joined the club two weeks earlier. Wilson was about to ruin one of the greatest throwing arms in baseball history when the pitcher, whose name was Dizzy Dean, brought him up short.

"Now Jimmy," said Dean, "You're a pretty good sort, and you wouldn't want the greatest pitcher that ever lived to go around poorly dressed, would you?" Dean was so convincing that Wilson told him to come around to his room and he'd lend him another silk shirt. And Diz took him up on the offer (Thorn, 1976, p. 116).

The moral to that story is this: Don't take on I players at their own game unless you're willing to lose your shirt.

Put it in Writing

When you have disagreements, look for alternate solutions. When you reach an agreement, nail down the specifics. Be sure both of you understand the who, what, when, where and how. Then put it in writing. The I person has a short memory for details.

When you're counseling I persons, it helps to give them opportunities to talk. They're prone to talk about themselves anyway, and this gives them a chance to look at what's bothering them. Ask them how they would solve their problems, and listen carefully to their responses. Pay particular attention to the feelings they express.

I persons often need nothing more than some opportunities to get things off their chests. At any rate, they draw their motivation from their relationships with others. The I player who has a good relationship with the coach will be motivated to give a good performance.

Remove Stress

I players tend to walk away from stressful situations. We've already noted Willie Mays' fear of failure in the 1951 National League play-offs. It had taken some managerial savvy to get Willie to report to the Giants from the Minneapolis farm team that year. It took even more to keep Willie's morale up during that rookie season. In dealing with Mays, Giants manager Leo Durocher showed that there was more to him than a hot temper and a penchant for kicking dirt on umpires' shoes.

When Willie was summoned to the majors, he was having a sensational season with the Minneapolis Millers, a farm team of the Giants. He tried to beg off going to New York. He told Durocher he wasn't ready for the majors, that he was afraid and didn't believe he could hit major-league pitching.

"What are you hitting now?" asked Durocher. Mays told him his batting average was .477.

Durocher wanted to know whether he could hit .250 for the Giants.

"Sure," said Willie. That didn't sound hard.

"Then get down here on the next plane," said Durocher. "We're playing in Philadelphia tonight and I want you there."

Hitting .250 was harder than Willie had expected. He just couldn't find the range in those first few games. After 25 trips to the plate, he had only one hit to his credit — a home run off Warren Spahn. The disconsolate rookie, contemplating his .040 batting average, sat next to his locker and cried.

When Durocher heard about it, he came to the locker room and put his arms around his center-fielder.

"What's the matter, son?" he asked.

"Mister Leo, I can't hit up here," sobbed Willie.

"What do you mean you can't hit? You're going to be a great ball player!"

"The pitching is just too fast for me here. They're going to send me back to Minneapolis."

Durocher would have none of that.

"Willie, see what's printed across my jersey? It says

Giants. As long as I'm the manager of the Giants, you're my center-fielder. You're here to stay. Stop worrying. With your talent, you're going to get plenty of hits."

Then Leo poured on the praise, mingled with solid advice:

> You're the greatest ball player I ever saw or ever hope to see. But Willie, you and your damn pull hitting. I don't know why you won't take the ball to right field. You can hit it into the bleachers here, over the fence, anywhere you want, yet you're still trying to pull the ball all the time. For you to do something wrong is an absolute disgrace. And I know you don't want to disgrace me, do you Willie? (Mays, 1988, p. 61)

Willie, of course, did get his hits — more than 3,200 of them over the next 22 seasons, including 660 home runs. But in that first season, under the stress of the major-league environment and a spectacular pennant race, the Say Hey kid was almost ready to head back to the minors. Leo Durocher pointed him toward greatness by proving that nice guys don't always finish last.

Set Positive Goals

Durocher may not have been able to identify the four basic behavior styles, but in dealing with Willie Mays, he showed that he knew instinctively how to deal with a disheartened I person. He assured his prize rookie that he had the stuff of greatness. He let him know what the challenge was. And he defined the behavior needed to surmount the challenge: Quit pulling the ball, Willie; spray those hits; go for the bleachers.

Notice that Leo didn't dwell on the negatives when he talked to Mays. It wasn't "How come you're 1 for 25 when you were hitting .477 with Minneapolis?" It was "If you can hit .477 there you can hit .250 here," and "You can hit it into the bleachers, over the fence, anywhere you want...."

When counseling I persons, keep the emphasis on the positive. They don't want to hear about how bad they've been. They want to hear about how good they can be. When talking to your slumping quarterback, don't talk to him about the number of interceptions he's thrown. Ask him how he'd like to increase the percentage of completions.

When you're talking to an I person, choose a non-threatening environment and keep the conversation congenial and unhurried.

Avoid complicated solutions. I persons don't deal with complexities very well. They'll follow your suggestions if the suggestions allow them to look good and don't call for a lot of boring follow-up or long-range commitment.

When they succeed in competition, or when they solve problems, let them know how happy you are for them.

THE SENSITIVITY ELEMENT

Of all the behavior types, Is are the most emotionally sensitive. They read things into body language, facial expression, tone of voice and the look in the eye. Is are even sensitive to colors! But mainly they are looking for acclaim, for recognition and for approval, and if they don't see it, their feelings may be easily hurt.

Again Willie Mays provides an example. Willie was in spring training with the Minneapolis Millers. During one game, Leo Durocher showed up, along with Horace Stoneham, the Giants' owner. Mays (1988) wrote:

> I was having a perfect day. If they were giving out MVP awards for spring-training games, I had just earned one. But after the seventh inning Durocher and Stoneham left. Just like that. I was shocked. Had I done something wrong? Was there a cutoff man I didn't throw to? Was there an extra base I could have stolen? I never found out. When the game was over I just sat in front of my locker, so tired I couldn't even shake my head. I felt like a raw rookie who had just flunked his only chance. I didn't see or talk to either of them the rest of the spring. (pp. 72-73)

To Stoneham and Durocher, it had been business as usual: You go to the farm club's park, you watch a promising young athlete, you take notes and you go on to the next phase of the job. To young Mays, it was an act of rejection, a failure to recognize his brilliant performance.

THE GRAND ENTRANCE FACTOR

I people love the grand entrance. Mays made Durocher an unwitting stage prop one evening when the Say Hey Kid decided to impress the youngsters in the modest neighborhood where he lived while he was struggling toward stardom.

Leo and Willie were scheduled to appear at a father-son banquet in Hackensack, New Jersey, one evening. Willie knew the manager planned to drive him to the event in his new Cadillac.

Willie passed the word to all the kids in the neighborhood that a chauffeur was to pick him up. When Durocher arrived, Willie opened the back door, climbed in and, in a voice loud enough to be heard the length of the block, said, "Okay, chauffeur, let's go."

Leo went along with the charade for a couple of blocks, then stopped and ordered Willie into the front seat (Mays, 1988, p. 54).

Colonel, Old Buddy

Pete Rose pulled something similar when he served a hitch in the Army after winning the Rookie of the Year award in the American League.

A colonel who was also a baseball fan had taken Pvt. Rose to a banquet in Louisville to show off the Army's prize recruit. The colonel treated the young athlete as a VIP instead of as a buck private.

They returned to Fort Knox in the colonel's car just as Pete's sergeant was lining up the platoon for evening formation. When he saw the car pull up, the sergeant yelled "Attention!" and even the second lieutenant in charge of them froze in a ramrod-straight stance.

Rose, taking in the situation, calmly opened the door and then leaned back into the car.

"Hey, thanks, Colonel," he said. "I'll see you later, old buddy."

The lieutenant snarled at Rose for failing to salute the colonel. Pete innocently shrugged it off.

"We've been together most of the afternoon. He's my friend. Like he's my buddy, sir" (Rose, 1970, p. 118-19).

The I person likes to please others. When a ball would land in an empty section of the stands and bounce back onto the playing field, Rose would throw it back into the stands so someone could claim it as a souvenir. It didn't necessarily please the Reds' management; baseballs cost money. But it increased Pete's popularity with the fans.

THE I AS COACH

The I coach needs to be aware that eagerness to please can be a drawback as well as an asset. The coach who plays a sub-par quarterback because that's what it takes to win the good will of a parent, an assistant coach or a member of the administration may find that good will has been bought at the expense of victory. And the price isn't worth it for the coach, for the player or for those the coach seeks to please.

MORE TIPS ON I PEOPLE

I persons can be motivated by providing them with friendly atmospheres, by freeing them from routine details, by giving them an opportunity to talk and by giving them opportunities to influence others. They don't like to work alone.

I people's weaknesses include a tendency to become involved in more projects than they have time to carry out. They may need the coach's help in setting priorities. They are impatient, bore easily and have short attention spans. They don't like being in ruts. The smart coach will try to vary the I person's routine, not requiring that the athlete or subordinate go through the same exercises over and over for long periods.

The biggest challenge with Retton, recalls Karolyi, was "to make her have patience and consistency, to have her hitting, hitting, hitting the same routines, repeating the same thing, which is sometimes very boring; it is not her style to spend too much time with one thing. Mary Lou liked to jump from one thing to another" (Retton and Karolyi, 1986, p. 91).

If I persons can't take in all the facts with one sweep of the eye, they'll make some broad assumptions and go with their gut feelings. They won't check out the details, leaving that boring job to others. They'll put things off.

I people like to look good and like to bask in the approval of others. Shower them with praise, and they'll do their best for you.

They are more likely to work well with people who are enthusiastic and optimistic. I persons don't like conflict. It's best to approach them in a non-aggressive way and to avoid getting into personal arguments with them. When they ask you how they're doing, give them a positive answer that emphasizes their progress and accomplishments, not their drawbacks and failures.

When you're delegating tasks to I people, make sure you both understand clearly what is expected. Have them report back to you at relatively short intervals. If you don't set up a timetable, they'll procrastinate and the task may not get done.

Coaches need to remind their I people that not everyone is going to like them. It's not because they're not interesting and it's not because they're lacking in charm. It's just that different people respond to different things, and some people just don't respond to the I person's personality. Tommy Lasorda would not have made friends with Billy Martin by hugging him and plying him with playful repartee.

I persons can learn to tone down the playful side of their nature in the presence of more serious-minded people. They can also accept the fact that their worth as individuals does not depend upon their ability to regale an audience. Runs and RBIs paid the rent for Willie Mays, not those flying caps.

D. DOMINANCE

- High ego strength
- Desire change
- Need direct answers
- Fear being taken advantage of
- Impatient
- Risk takers
- Not easily discouraged

I. INFLUENCING

- Emotional
- People oriented
- Need Social Recognition
- Fear loss of social approval
- Disorganized
- Memory for color
- High verbal skills

S. STEADINESS

- **Best listeners**
- **Results orientated**
- **Need procedures**
- **Fear loss of security**
- **Possessive**
- **Quiet, but witty**
- **Keeps emotions hidden**

C. COMPLIANCE

- Accurate
- Diplomatic
- Needs to do things right way
- Fear criticism about their work
- Can be too critical
- Seeks "ideal" mate
- Like charts, graphs, figures

4

"S" is for Steadiness

As you cull through the commentaries on baseball personalities, one name keeps cropping up, nearly always in a nice-guy context. The name is Joe DiMaggio.

Billy Martin remembered him as the superstar who took a brash, pugnacious rookie under his wing and befriended him when other teammates were shunning the youngster as a misfit who didn't conform to the Yankee image. Pete Rose remembers the feeling of awe when Joe invited him to go with him to Vietnam to bolster the morale of the American troops there. To Willie Mays, Joe DiMaggio was the boyhood hero whose exploits Willie followed closely even after he had embarked on a professional baseball career of his own. Joe later became an admirer of Willie, whose achievements with bat and glove eventually elevated him to the same plateau of greatness as the magnificent Yankee slugger.

And George Plimpton (1974) described how Henry Aaron stole bases in "that sort of gliding deceptive way that was never terribly exciting to watch but was like Joe DiMaggio's — effective and always done at just the right time so it meant something in the outcome of the game" (p. 65).

THE ONE TO COUNT ON

What behavior style did the Yankee Clipper exemplify? He was not a D. DiMaggio was not one of those win-at-all-costs players in the mold of Billy Martin. Joe was graceful in victory and defeat. He never did anything that would be a disgrace to his pinstripes. And the cliché was that he looked better striking out than most players looked swatting a home run.

Nor was he one to boast about his exploits in the manner of Reggie Jackson. He was too sensitive to the feelings of others to be a D. In all those years when DiMaggio and Ted Williams were running neck and neck in home run output and batting averages, you never heard Joe utter a taunting or belittling remark about his rival in Fenway Park.

Joe was not a showman in the mold of Pete Rose or Willie Mays. He would never wear a loose-fitting cap, as Mays did, just so it would fall off and draw attention to himself. And while Rose specialized in milking excitement even from a base on balls, DiMaggio specialized in making even the most difficult outfield catches look easy and routine.

Joe must be a behavioral S, the epitome of steadiness and stability.

His greatest accomplishment on the field was a monument to steady performance: He hit safely in 56 consecutive games. No player before or since has come close to that mark.

Off the field, too, Joe was a model of loyalty and dependability. It was steady Joe who stayed loyal to the unhappy Marilyn Monroe, even after their marriage was long over; it was Joe who took charge of funeral arrangements for the tragic beauty.

Steady Aaron

Henry Aaron provides another fine example of an S person. Author Plimpton (1974) captures Hammerin' Hank's essential nature in describing his record-shattering 715th career home run: "It was a simple act by an unassuming man, which touched an enormous circle of people, indeed an entire country" (p. 1).

If you're looking for someone with the ability to get along with all types of people, go for the S style. They are the people who want to be liked and who devote their best efforts to pleasing others. They are agreeable, supportive, and loyal. An S person is the least likely to burst into a temper tantrum, throw a chair across a gym floor, slam dunk a referee, or get involved in a dugout fracas.

S people are like Wilma Rudolph, Ed Temple's magnificent 6-foot running star who became a celebrity after her performance in the 1960 Olympics at Rome.

"Rudolph had such a pleasant personality and smile, and she was just herself, so I suppose this helped people to relate to her so easily," wrote Temple (1980, p. 84).

They're people like Pie Traynor, who was known throughout the National League as a perfect gentleman, never one to use profanity or to lose his temper.

Once umpire Bill Klem ejected him from a game for no apparent reason. After the game, reporters asked Klem why he did it.

"He wasn't feeling well," replied Klem.

The reporters didn't understand. Nothing appeared to be wrong with Traynor.

"That's what he told me," said Klem. "He came up to me like the perfect gentleman he is and said, 'Mr. Klem, I'm sick and tired of your stupid decisions.'"

They're people like Michael Jordan, the magnificent flying machine of the Chicago Bulls who, according to teammate Orlando Woolridge, "makes everyone around him look good" while performing spectacular feats on the basketball court.

S persons are good listeners. If you give them a set of instructions to carry out, they'll follow them and turn in a good job in the bargain. Consistency is a major virtue with them.

THE SILENT TYPE

Author Michael Seidel (1988) was describing the S behavior style when he characterized the community of heroes into which DiMaggio stepped during the era just prior to World War II:

"Tall, silent, to a notable extent shy, figures of consistency, endurance, and understated style — those represented, say, by the mild-mannered Clark Kent or portrayed by Gary Cooper and Jimmy Stewart in the movies" (pp. 1-2).

Note too the way Henry Aaron's performance lives up to the criteria for an S person.

Aaron holds the all-time record for career home runs — 755 in 21 seasons. Yet you'd never know it from looking at his year-by-year totals. Babe Ruth, whose long-standing record Aaron beat, had four seasons in which he hit 50 or more home runs, culminating in his spectacular 1927 total of 60.

Ruth was the first slugger to top 50 homers in a season, but several others followed. Hack Wilson struck 56 for the Cubs in 1930, Jimmy Foxx hit 58 for the A's in 1932 and Hank Greenberg of the Tigers matched him in 1938. The Pirates' Ralph Kiner and the Giants' John Mize each hit 51 in 1947, and Kiner came back with 54 in 1949.

In Aaron's own time, Willie Mays hit 51 home runs for the Giants in 1954 while Mickey Mantle hit 52 for the Yankees in 1956 and Roger Maris, the other half of the M&M twins, set the all-time record with 61 in 1961.

Aaron's career high was 45 home runs in 1962, and even then Mays beat him out for the National League title with 49 homers, while Harmon Killebrew led the American League with 48. But Aaron kept slugging away, season after season. It wasn't until 1957, his fourth year in the majors, that his season total topped 30. After that, he averaged 37.6 home runs per season for the next 10 years. Then he averaged 39.4 for the succeeding five.

Aaron was hurt when he failed to win the "Athlete of the Decade" recognition for the '70s after surpassing Ruth's record. But in truth, Aaron's accomplishments were spread rather evenly over parts of three decades, and he didn't dominate any of them.

THE S VALUES

As a loyal, supportive S person, Aaron didn't hit home runs for the glory of it. He did it to help his team win. The home run that gave him the most satisfaction was not No. 715 — the one that broke Ruth's record — but No. 109, the one he hit in the 11th inning of a game against the St. Louis Cardinals in 1957. That blow won the pennant for the Milwaukee Braves.

Aaron would later say that if his team was behind 2-1 in the eighth inning, he'd go for the home run; that's what was needed to win. If the team was ahead 8-1, he'd also go for the home run; the game was on ice, and Henry might as well fatten his total. Otherwise, he'd do what he could to help the team: "First you play baseball; then you play to win; then you try for home runs" (Plimpton, 1974, p. 66).

S persons don't necessarily live to win; they live to serve others, thereby winning their affection and respect.

"I don't want to overshadow anyone," said Michael Jordan after he joined the down-and-out Chicago Bulls. "I'm playing my natural game, and I think I'm establishing myself, gaining the respect of the players. Maybe my personality can inspire the other guys."

His personality was biased toward serving others. Once, when his college roommate went home for a weekend to visit a sick aunt, Jordan cleaned the entire apartment, made his roommate's bed and tidied up his closet. On a Halloween night when Jordan couldn't be home, he left a note for trick-or-treaters to come back later. When they did, he treated them to hamburgers (Krugel, 1989, pp. 40-41).

Whatever S players do, they try to do it well, hoping to win approval. When the approval comes, it need not be extravagant or effusive. Sincere praise is the S person's goal.

When President Nixon called Hank Aaron to congratulate him on No. 715, Hank's response was low-key and modest: "Thank you very much, Mr. President. Yeah, it was a long struggle, but I finally made it."

When television sportscaster Pat O'Brien, marveling at Michael Jordan's basketball aerobatics, made the half-statement, half-question, "You really can fly?" Jordan replied modestly, "Well, maybe a little bit."

S players shun the hell-for-leather pace of their D teammates and the showboating theatrics of the I performers. They may even be self-effacing.

Tony Gwynn, San Diego's three-time National League batting champion, was like that. When Gwynn's performance won the game for the Padres, the post-game interviews would always find him sharing the credit with teammates.

Mickey Mantle was another self-effacing S person. His teammates liked him and admired him, not only because he was good-natured and unassuming, but also because he was extremely loyal to the team. Only the players knew the agony Mantle endured, playing with bad legs that would have had less dedicated players on the bench or in the hospital.

S persons seek security and long-term stability. The unknown may intrigue them, but they're more comfortable with the tried and true. Hank Aaron was not the kind of hitter who kept an assortment of bats on hand. He had one bat that he liked, and he stuck with it. He kept only one other in the dugout as a spare, just in case he cracked the regular bat.

Let Actions do the Talking

S persons are not the kind of people who march boldly into the boss's office and demand the raises they deserve. Instead, they believe that their accomplishments speak for themselves. They'll wait for the boss to notice how well they're doing.

When that recognition doesn't come, they feel hurt. That's how Laker star Michael Cooper felt during contract negotiations in the summer of 1986.

Pat Riley (1988) wrote that "[l]oyalty and demonstrated affection are two of Michael's highest values" (p. 43). Cooper didn't think the Lakers were being very loyal and affectionate during the negotiations. They weren't offering him what he thought his athletic performance had earned, and they had even suggested he become a free agent to see what salary he could command; if the Lakers thought he was worth that salary, they would match it.

That kind of attitude suggested to Cooper that the Lakers didn't value him very much as a person.

"Some people, if you give them a wonderful contract, will suddenly go soft," Riley observed. "Michael is the opposite. Let him know how much you care and he'll get stronger and stronger. That's the way his heart works."

For a while, Cooper decided to "show them." He would play so well that some other team would outbid the Lakers for his services. That attitude is typical of S persons. When they are hurt by the feeling of rejection, they'll either try harder or withdraw. In this case, Cooper was doing both: He was trying harder to gain the approval of some other team, and he was withdrawing from his relationship with the Lakers.

Riley's handling of Coop was the classic way of dealing with an S person. He pointed out how comfortable Michael had been with the Lakers: "For the $100,000 more you want, or whatever, don't throw away seven years of what you have built up. You're a highly respected player here, well known in your community." He brought in the family ties: "Your family's from this area." He appealed to team loyalty: "You're in Los Angeles, you're on a championship team, you play with players you love." He played on the S person's fear of the unknown: "Some other team might give you everything on your list and you'd walk into a situation that you're going to hate" (Riley, 1988, p. 44).

This time around, Cooper eventually decided that it was better to stick with the team he knew and liked than to risk jumping into an environment that might not be so congenial. In October of that year, at the Lakers' Media Day event, Michael showed up in his Laker uniform. He was still unsigned, but he and management were close to agreement, and he wanted to demonstrate loyalty to the team, as a good S should.

Use Reason, Not Instinct

S people rely more on deductive reasoning than on instinct. They think more than they feel. When Aaron knew the pitcher he was going to be facing, he would analyze the foe. He would find out what pitches he threw best. Instead of waiting to see which of the pitches was coming at him, Aaron would decide in advance which pitch he would be waiting for. He would eliminate the other pitches from consideration. When the chosen pitch did come, Hank was ready for it.

Hank followed this system religiously. The hurler with a limited repertoire of pitches was in trouble when Aaron stepped up. The pitcher with a good variety of throws found him easier to handle.

Go by Procedure

S persons are sticklers for procedure. They don't like to experiment and innovate. When I drive to and from a hotel to a conference center in a strange city, I may take one route in the morning and a different route in the evening. Getting *there* is what matters, not *getting* there; that's the I behavior at work.

The S person will find the "correct" route and stick with it.

The difference between S and I can be noticed in the classroom too. As a junior-high-school student, I once had a problem with math. The math teacher suggested an after-class meeting. At the appointed time, the teacher returned the corrected homework papers, which looked as though someone had bled on them.

The problem was not with the answers, the teacher said. They were correct. But the wrong procedure had been used to arrive at the answers.

That was an S person trying to teach an I person.

Watch the Base, Not the Ball

Hank Aaron went by procedure. When Babe Ruth or Reggie Jackson or Willie Mays hit a home run, you could see them savoring it. Their eyes would follow the ball until it landed in the stands or cleared the outfield fence.

Not Aaron. He says he never saw a home-run ball land.

"That's not what I'm supposed to do," he said. "I've seen guys miss first base looking to see where the ball went. My job is to get down to first base and touch it. Looking at the ball going over the fence isn't going to help" (Plimpton, 1974, p. 15).

Hank followed procedure even when the run was in the bag. Maybe he was aware of what happened to the New York Mets in 1962 when "Marvelous Marv" Throneberry slugged one into the farthest corner of the Polo Grounds. Throneberry slid into third with a triple, but the other side claimed he failed to touch second base. The umpire agreed, and Marv was called out.

A livid Casey Stengel stormed out to express his considered view of the umpire's judgment.

"Don't bother, Casey," said the Mets' first-base coach. "He didn't touch first either" (Thorn, 1976, p. 195). Marvelous Marv was not an S.

Take One Step at a Time

The successful coach will remember the S players' preferences for doing things by the numbers. They want to know what procedure to follow: First hit the ball, then run to first, then touch the bag. Teach them the procedure one step at a time.

Because S people set high standards for themselves, they are reluctant to embark on any task they haven't mastered. Therefore, they'll want you to lead them through step by step, and they will not want to move on until they're sure they're good at it. I people will plunge right in before they know all the fine points and pitfalls. "I can do it!" they'll say. But not S people. They're like Michael Jordan before the 1985 NBA all-star game.

"I've got some things I haven't done in front of people yet," he said, "but I've got to get out and practice them" (Krugel, 1989, p. 5). Jordan's feats were the wonder of the basketball court, but he was unwilling to "show off" new techniques until he was sure he had mastered them.

When you're teaching S players something new, it helps to provide them with an outline, a working timetable or step-by-step instructions. They prefer hands-on training, and they'll want you to start at the beginning and walk them through.

When Billy Martin reported to the New York Yankees as a rookie, the great Frank Crosetti was instructing the young infielders on the proper way to make a double play. The brash Martin already knew how, and he proceeded to instruct Crosetti — in a way that was different from Crosetti's way. An S person would never do that.

SOME S WEAKNESSES

S persons are so devoted to procedure that they may persist in following it even when it's no longer necessary. Once a task has been mastered, it's usually possible to eliminate certain steps, to take certain short cuts, and still do it well. The S person tends to continue in the routine as it was learned.

Henry Aaron learned that the most important thing to do after you've hit the ball is to go down to first and make sure you touch the base. He never accepted the fact that you could break the routine long enough to watch the ball sail out of the park and still collect your run.

Procedures Followed — No Matter What

Because of this devotion to procedure, S people make good tutors. They are well organized, and they enjoy helping others to be organized. When they undertake a task, they get all their equipment together, put it in precisely the order that it will be used, and only then start to work.

Coach S will tell her softball team, "Okay, here's how we're going to do it. We're going to do step one, which is basic base-running. Step two, we're going to learn the hit-and-run. Step three, we're going to learn how to steal second."

The impatient I athlete will say, "Let's take up base-stealing first."

And Coach S will inform her, "Sorry. We're going by procedure. First, you learn to run the baselines...."

If you need somebody to write a procedural manual, you know where to look.

Messages Coded

One thing that often causes misunderstandings between S persons and their D and C colleagues is the S person's preference for speaking indirectly. S people are sensitive to nuances in speech and body language and expect associates to get their message even when the message is in code. They fear that straight talk may give offense and cause the hearer not to like them. D and C people understand straight talk. They don't take hints.

At a Coaches' All-Star game in Lubbock, Texas, Bo Schembechler, then the University of Michigan football coach, was holding a session with the East's offensive team. Joe Gilliam, quarterback for Tennessee State, and later for the Pittsburgh Steelers, lit a cigarette.

Schembechler didn't allow that among his Michigan athletes, but he was uncharacteristically timid in dealing with the situation among all-stars who didn't normally play for him.

An S coach would have said something like this:

> I know that you guys want to win, and winners don't throw away the edge to the other team. They don't indulge in habits that might be unhealthy for them and for their teammates. When you see something blowing from their nostrils, you know it's a cold day and they're exhaling vapor. So let's just clear the air and go out there and win.

The S coach would have said that and Joe Gilliam would have continued to smoke.

Had this been his Michigan team, Schembechler would have put the message across in memorable style. But this time, Bo showed the seldom-seen S side of his personality and called in the head coach, a fellow the folks in Alabama called Bear Bryant.

"Hey," said Bo. "I want to tell you something. I'm not teaching football to any son of a gun smoking a cigarette."

Bear gave Bo a wave of the hand and walked confidently into the meeting.

"Hello, men," he said. "I want to tell you something: We're here to play football. I don't care what you do when we're not playing football, but when you're in a meeting, or practicing, we'll do things the way they're supposed to be." He paused for effect. "And there ain't going to be no smoking in here. Now, Gilliam, you get that cigarette out."

Gilliam put out his cigarette (Schembechler and Albom, 1989, p. 117).

Niceness Personified

The S person's motivation may be a mystifying thing to other behavior types. To the S, pleasing others is more important than winning. If you see a Church League mother cheering her neighbor's daughter in a field hockey game, even though the neighbor's daughter just blocked a goal attempt by her own daughter, you'll know the cheers are coming from the throat of an S.

To the D person, whose objective is to win, win, win, such behavior is blasphemous, to say the least. Billy Martin once had to leave the ballpark and hole up in a hotel bar in order to get around his boss's insistence on being nice even when it hurt.

As manager for the Oakland Athletics, Martin had been thrown out of the game for speaking too directly to an umpire. Third-base coach Clete Boyer had to take over in his absence. Billy did what any D person would recognize as the natural thing: He went to his office, tuned in the game on his television set, got Boyer on the telephone and proceeded to manage his team.

As Martin (1987) put it, "Cheating is as much a part of the game as score cards and hot dogs, although I really don't look upon it as cheating as much as getting any edge you can" (p. 157).

It was an attitude Billy was never able to sell to the A's owner, Roy Eisenhardt. When Eisenhardt found Billy circumventing the umpire's decision, to the benefit of the A's, the owner reproached him: "Oh no, Billy. That's not right. You were thrown out of this game. I don't want you doing that."

Billy humbly switched off the set, left the stadium, ducked into a nearby Holiday Inn and headed for the bar. There he found the game in progress on the television set. He found a telephone within easy viewing distance of the screen, got through to Boyer and proceeded to manage his team.

"Roy is a very honorable man," lamented Billy. "Too honest to be a baseball owner. What a pair we were" (Martin, 1987, pp. 157-58).

S people's need to be nice can be their undoing. Martin thought Red Sox Manager Johnny McNamara's decision to leave Bill Buckner in the game in the ninth inning of the sixth game of the 1986 World Series was based on sentiment, and it cost the Red Sox the game and the series (Martin, 1987, pp. 240-41).

Yogi Got No Respect

Martin (1987) spoke well of Yogi Berra, though Yogi was not Martin's kind of manager.

"Yogi is the easygoing, low-key type," he wrote. "... I'm tough on players. Yogi is not. I'm not saying my way is right and Yogi's is wrong, but it's different, and every manager has to get his players to do things his way. My way has been very successful for me" (pp. 240-41).

Jim Bouton and Bill Veeck both agree that Yogi's reputation as a clown is largely the product of fiction and that Berra, in Veeck's (1973) words, was "a friendly guy, a regular guy, a neighborhood guy without sham or pretension" (p. 90).

But this nice disposition didn't win pennants for Berra teams. As Bouton (1973a) put it, "The players never completely respected Yogi. He was always 'good old Yog,' who was thought to be in over his head as a coach" (p. 106).

S people's chief problem as coaches is their aversion to conflict. The desire to be Mr. or Ms. Nice puts them in Yogi Berra's position: The players like them, but don't respect them. S coaches need to recognize that they're never going to be liked by everybody, and it's no tragedy if they aren't. It is important that discipline be maintained, whether on the coaching staff or on the team.

Habits Formed

Another thing the S person needs to guard against is resistance to change. S people become comfortable in their routines. They cherish the old way of doing things. Aaron was so averse to change that he even used the toeholds at the plate that had been dug by Tony Kubek, who preceded him in the batting order. When Hank's average started to slide, he would take Kubek to the plate with a tape measure to see whether his teammate had altered his stance.

But too much adherence to routine can be a bad thing. Without change, there's no progress. Stagnation sets in, and there goes the will to win.

MEETING S NEEDS

There are of course, many strengths in S persons. By taking their values and needs into account, you can go a long way toward creating the optimal setting for working with S people.

Family Ties

Family relationships are important to S people.

Pat Riley (1988) was moved to write about his appreciation for the solid family values of Michael and Wanda Cooper on his Los Angeles Lakers.

"Coop...sees the link between family stability and championship performance," penned the coach. Once Cooper told him, "The only way you can play basketball at this level, to the maximum of your ability, is if you go out feeling loose. You can't compete with stress or worries tightening you up" (p. 135). And to a player such as Cooper, a stable family life is essential to a stress-free life.

In the midst of the Lakers' championship drive of 1987, a player came to Riley and apologized for performing at less than 100%, blaming it on family problems. Riley replied, "The main thing I want you to do is get your family stuff together" (Riley, 1988, p. 136).

Michael Jordan, too, exemplifies the family orientation of the S athlete. One of his first acts as a pro was to buy his parents in North Carolina a satellite disc so they could watch his games wherever he played. Jordan values his parents' opinions. When he bought his own home, he flew them to Chicago to help decorate it (Krugel, 1989, p. 4).

S persons are overly tolerant, but they can also hold grudges. They nurse their anger inwardly instead of letting it out in a burst of rage, as a D person might do.

Security

Their great fear is a loss of security. They want things to stay calm and stable around them. If change is in the offing, S persons need to be prepared for it. They need to be assured that along with the change, some things will remain stable. Then they can cling to the familiar while they get their bearings among the changes.

This aversion to change may imbue the S person with a sense of possessiveness. If you go to a seminar or meeting in which no seats are assigned, note which persons will return to the seats they left after a break. Most of those persons will be Ss. They are returning to "their" seats. Athletes may also develop this sense of possessiveness about the lockers they use or the positions they play. Before ordering a change, the coach needs to give them plenty of advance notice so that they can adjust to the new position, or the new location.

Stable Environment

The ideal environment for S people provides plenty of stability, security, expressions of appreciation, affirmation for jobs well done, and freedom from conflict.

S persons need to be encouraged to take the initiative. The coach can help them by suggesting they plan a strategy and stick to it. Because S people value relationships above winning, the coach will need to establish a warm relationship toward them. Then they'll want to win to preserve their relationship with the coach.

Since S people tend to hold hostile feelings inside, the coach needs to encourage them to express their feelings, even if they disagree with the coach. Whenever an S person faces a confrontation, or needs to confront someone, the coach should be supportive. Conflict pains the peace-loving S, but the problem won't go away if it isn't faced.

WORKING WITH Ss

S persons become cooperative members of the coaching staff. They bring natural planning skills, a consistent pace and a desire to fit in. They enjoy working with others on a first-name basis. They will not make waves and will not stir up conflict.

S persons may feel they're bearing the brunt of the work load, but they'll keep these thoughts to themselves. Although they'll observe the way others perform, they are unlikely to criticize them.

When you're praising an S person, make sure it's genuine praise. They can sense phony compliments, and they resent them. Mention specific qualities, not just abstract virtues. Praise their teamwork, their dependability.

When counseling them, remember that S people rarely come right out and say what they mean. Take plenty of time to draw them out. Listen carefully to their responses.

If the S person is fearful of impending change, try to show how the change will be beneficial. Emphasize, too, the things that will remain unchanged. The S person needs something familiar to cling to.

Criticize Carefully

Criticizing S people can be a delicate undertaking. They take criticism personally, and they bruise easily. Be sure they know that you're criticizing a specific behavior and not the person. You may mean to say, "Sonja, I see what's wrong with your swing," but Sonja may take it to mean, "I see what's wrong with you."

The way to avoid this is to focus on the procedure you want to correct.

Coach Diane Dempsey approached Sarah Scott, who played third base for her softball team:

> Sarah, you're too wishy-washy in everything you do. You can't make up your mind which bat to use, which pitch to swing at or which base to throw to. Look at the way you're fielding those grounders. You're hanging back and letting the ball come to you. That's why so many runners are getting on base and so many runs are scoring against us.

Sarah immediately felt rejected and unwanted as a person. She was wishy-washy, therefore inadequate, and therefore unlikable.

Had Coach Dempsey determined the behavior styles of her players, she would have known that Sarah was an S and that this critical approach was almost guaranteed to destroy Sarah's morale and cause her to give up.

She would have approached Sarah in this way:

> Hi Sarah. It's nice to have a steady, level-headed person like you at third base. You think before you act, which is good. You can be the anchor for our infield. In watching you play the position, though, I think I've spotted a way to increase your put-outs and assists. I've noticed that when a grounder is hit your way, you figure out where it's going and you wait for it. Why don't you

try charging the ball? Then stop just before it reaches you, put your glove down and field it. When you do that, you may get a step or two advantage on the runner.

By using this approach, Coach Dempsey has not criticized Sarah as a person. In fact, she has complimented her good qualities. She has focused on Sarah's procedure and has suggested a way to improve it. Sarah no longer feels there is something wrong with her. Instead, she feels the coach really likes her, and she is motivated to do something that will increase her approval rating in the coach's eyes.

Take One Problem at a Time

Note too that in dealing with an S person, you deal with only one problem at a time. The immediate concern was Sarah's fielding, not her batting, her throwing or her general indecisiveness. Knowing that Sarah is an S person, Coach Dempsey would make sure that Sarah had learned the technique of fielding the ball before moving on to the question of where and how to throw. She would make sure that Sarah's defensive problems were solved before concentrating on her technique at the plate.

When dealing with S people, the coach may do most of the talking because Ss feel uncomfortable in the spotlight. But the coach should encourage S players to contribute their own suggestions. When you have a better idea, instead of directly contradicting the player, just point out that you're looking for ways to make things more pleasant for the individual.

As staffers, S people may be inclined to do everything themselves, believing that's the best way to get things done. They should be encouraged to delegate. You can provide this encouragement by appealing to their sense of loyalty, teamwork and sportsmanship.

When assigning them tasks, tell them what needs to be done, give them deadlines to meet and explain why it's important to do it the way you want it done.

IF YOU'RE AN S

If you're an S person, you may want to develop your initiative by challenging yourself. Take on a bit more than you feel comfortable with. Plunge into tasks more quickly than you're accustomed to doing. Speak up more than usual; let people know how you really feel. And try to develop a thicker skin so negative comments from your colleagues don't land you in the pits. Look for new ways to do things. The rut may feel comfortable, but if you're going to grow you need to plow new furrows occasionally.

Also, learn to delegate. You multiply your own power when you learn to let others do things for you. A shortstop can't make every put-out unassisted. Most of the time he has to throw to the second-baseman. The best quarterback in the business has to hand the ball off or throw it to a receiver more often than he runs with it. Coaches, too, have to know when to run with the ball and when to hand off or pass. S coaches, in particular, need to combat the tendency to do everything themselves.

Just as important, learn to say no. The S person will find the occasional negative to be the leavening that adds flavor to the personality. Umpires have to call balls as well as strikes. Leaders have to impose sanctions as well as bestow rewards.

Can an S person be a true leader?

You bet. During World War II, when a general was needed to deal simultaneously with the American president, the British prime minister and their retinue of military and civilian advisers; when a competent organizer was needed to plan the greatest invasion in human history; when a deft hand was needed to deal with the temperamental George Patton and the egotistical Bernard Montgomery, the leaders of the world's greatest democracies chose an S person to do the job.

Dwight Eisenhower came through.

D. DOMINANCE

- High ego strength
- Desire change
- Need direct answers
- Fear being taken advantage of
- Impatient
- Risk takers
- Not easily discouraged

I. INFLUENCING

- Emotional
- People oriented
- Need Social Recognition
- Fear loss of social approval
- Disorganized
- Memory for color
- High verbal skills

S. STEADINESS

- Best listeners
- Results orientated
- Need procedures
- Fear loss of security
- Possessive
- Quiet, but witty
- Keeps emotions hidden

C. COMPLIANCE

- Accurate
- Diplomatic
- Needs to do things right way
- Fear criticism about their work
- Can be too critical
- Seeks "ideal" mate
- Like charts, graphs, figures

5

"C" is for Cautious Compliance

A 10-year-old girl was asked to submit an essay for her 5th-grade class on the subject, "What I Want To Do With the Rest of My Life."

She wrote:

> I want to see all the countries in the world and learn all the languages. I want to have thousands of friends and I want all my friends to be different. I want to play six instruments. I want to be the best in the world at two things. I want to be a great athlete and I want to be a great surgeon.

Noting that she had only 70 years left if she expected to do all this by the time she was 80, she concluded:

> I need to practice very hard every day. I need to sleep as little as possible. I need to read at least one major book every week. And I need to remember that my 70 years are going to go by too quickly. (Nyad, 1978, p. 66)

About halfway through those 70 years, Diana Nyad hadn't attained every one of those goals, but she had learned several languages, traveled around the world at least six times, climbed Mount Kilimanjaro, achieved Phi Beta Kappa in college, studied comparative literature at the doctoral level and become a writer and lecturer.

And oh yes, she had become a great athlete.

In her quest for athletic greatness, Diana was not driven by the D person's need to win, to dominate, to control. She was not spurred by the I person's hunger for acclaim or the need to shine brighter than her opponents. She was not motivated by the S person's desire to please others.

Diana was driven by her consuming passion for perfection: the constant need to meet her own high standards of performance. Why else would she have chosen a sport such as long-distance swimming, where the cheering crowds are far away, the pain is only too present and the material rewards barely match the expenses? Why else would she have chosen to swim Lake Ontario, not the "easy" way — from the south shore to the north — but from the north shore to the south, where the last five miles is a grueling struggle against the current of the Niagara River? And why, having completed that exhausting ordeal, would she have plunged back in after a 10-minute "rest" and swum till she was unconscious, trying to make it a round trip?

When Diana was a child, she kept two posters on her bedroom wall, each with a slogan. One read, "There is no gain without pain." The other read, "A diamond is a lump of coal that stuck with it" (Nyad, 1978, p. 66). Diana was determined to endure whatever pain was necessary until she perceived a diamond gleaming where once there had been a lump of coal.

Diana fits the description of a C person, the cerebral perfectionist whose aim is compliance with her own high standards. The C can also stand for "cautious" in the sense that a C person will cautiously refrain from acting until all the facts are in and analyzed.

THE MATCHLESS FEAT

Diana's ultimate goal — and the goal of other C persons involved in public performances — was to leave observers feeling they had witnessed a matchless feat.

Listen to her savoring her victory over Lake Ontario after her 32-mile swim from north to south:

> At 1:20 a.m. I touch the shore after 18 hours and 20 minutes of nonstop swimming. I am frozen, my legs can't

support me, my arms feel bruised from battling the waves for so many hours, and even though I am psyching up for the return trip, which must begin in ten minutes...I allow myself a moment of glory. I know that I am the first and only person, male or female, to have crossed this brutal beast north to south. (Nyad, 1978, p. 13)

Listen to her describing the wonderment of the spectators at the end of a marathon feat:

They gather by the thousands on the shores of Argentinean rivers, Australian oceans and Canadian lakes to stare at an individual who has pushed herself beyond every conceivable limit. They are fascinated by this thoroughly spent body, this 110% effort, especially in an era when motivation is deteriorating and limitations are rarely pushed. They are willing to wait long hours for one quick glimpse of a most extreme moment. Sometimes I walk out of a swim on my own, often I need help, and occasionally I go by the ambulance stretcher. They are always there. The men yell "Bravo, Diana," "Fantastic!" "Brave young woman!" And the women just stare. Incredulous, awe-filled, envious stares. The utter exhaustion, and the courage it conveys, seems to be an inspiration to everyone who witnesses it. (Nyad, 1978, pp. 14-15)

Listen to her ultimate ambition:

I want to do something unprecedented in the world of sports — something so outrageously difficult it would go unmatched for many many years. I want to bid my love affair with marathon swimming a spectacular farewell. I want to accomplish the unimaginable. (Nyad, 1978, p.154)

Diana's sheer commitment and rage for perfection are rarely matched on the field, on the court, in the arena or in the water. But her basic behavior style is matched by many others. About 35% of us are C people, and a high percentage of athletes follow this behavior style. Wayne Gretsky on the hockey ice and Larry Bird on the basketball court hone themselves for spectacular performances toward the goal of perfection. On the tennis court, Diana sees reflections of her own single-minded concentration in the performances of Chris Evert and Bjorn Borg. On the baseball diamond, Ted Williams offers an interesting contrast with his S-like contemporary, Joe DiMaggio.

Let us examine some of the clues that alert us to the fact that we're dealing with a C person.

QUALITY CONTROL

This behavior style can be characterized in two words: quality control. C people aim for accuracy and consistency. When Diana Nyad swam, she could gauge the distance traveled by the number of strokes she made. She would repeat over and over simple songs such as "Row, Row, Row Your Boat," or "Frere Jacques" (in three languages), measuring the distance she covered by the number of times she sang the song (Nyad, 1978, p. 113).

A C person believes in checking and double-checking. In their book *People Smart*, authors Tony Allessandra and Michael O'Connor (1990) describe the way airplane pilots go down their pre-flight checklists:

The D person will delegate the job to another crew member.

The I person will often get involved in conversation with a fellow crew member, underestimate the time required to complete the list and hurry through it at the last minute.

The S person will go down the checklist step by step, giving equal attention to every item on the list.

The C person will first go to the most critical items on the list and, having completed them, will then go to the less-critical items (p. 119).

This attention to detail is where the C for caution enters the picture. The C person doesn't want to commit to a course of action until all the relevant information has been received, analyzed and weighed. Other behavior types may find this tendency irritating and may view the C person as indecisive.

That doesn't bother C people. Unlike the Is and Ss, they don't measure their success by the approval of others. Neither do they measure it by the D person's standards of winning or losing. It's the quality that counts.

As the mother of Olympic runner Brenda Morehead put it, "Don't want to win; want a record!" (Temple, 1980, p. 54).

With Joe Paterno, too, winning was not enough. When he took over as head coach at Penn State, he didn't just aspire to be more successful than his predecessor. Even being the best coach in Penn State history wasn't enough: "I didn't see why I should leave room in the number one spot for sharing with Bear Bryant or Vince Lombardi or anybody else" (Paterno, 1989, p. 94).

PERFECTION (MINUS .0004)

It was this yearning for excellence that drove Ted Williams to the top ranks of major-league hitters. In the final week of the 1941 season, Williams seemed to have a .400 season locked up. Then a rookie pitcher handcuffed him three times in a single game and his average dipped to .3996. With a doubleheader coming up and the Red Sox out of the pennant race, manager Joe Cronin offered to let Ted ride the bench. He knew that in the record books Ted's average would be rounded off to an even .400.

But Williams would have none of it. If .400 represents perfection, .3996 is perfection minus .0004. The consummate slugger played both games, got six hits and ended the season with an honest .406 batting average.

Ted's reaction to this achievement was typical of the perfectionist: "Well, suppose your boss gave you ten jobs to do and you only did four of them right," he told one interviewer. "How would you feel?"(Thorn, 1976, p. 141).

Notice the lack of braggadocio here. Henry Aaron was low-key too in his reaction to home run No. 715. "Yeah, it was a long struggle, but I finally made it," he told President Nixon. But notice the subtle difference between the S person's self-deprecation and the C person's perfectionism: For Aaron, passing Ruth's record marked the end of a long, plodding struggle. There was nothing spectacular about it; it was just a case of steady performance. For Williams, hitting .406 was an achievement to be measured against perfection. It was a splendid accomplishment indeed, but it was only a little better than 40% of perfection.

Joe Paterno (1989) took a similar view of achievements

when it came to his Penn State teams. "A Penn Stater doesn't have to let the whole world know, by putting six Nittany Lions on his helmet, that he made six big plays," he wrote. "When he scores a touchdown, he doesn't dance and go berserk in the end zone. When a Penn Stater goes on that field, he expects to make a touchdown" (pp. 129-130).

Joe McCarthy, one of the most successful baseball managers in history, was another perfectionist. McCarthy took over the Yankees in 1931, and that year his power-laden team played the minor-league Milwaukee Brewers an exhibition game. Murderer's Row was still in business, and the Yanks won it 19-1.

"How'd you like that? Pretty good, huh?" asked Jimmy Reese, a second baseman just up from the Pacific Coast League.

"Against a bunch of bums like that, you should've made 30 runs," grumbled McCarthy (Fitzgerald, 1973, p. 264).

TED vs. JOE

Throughout the late '30s and '40s, DiMaggio and Williams treated the baseball world to a rare display of batting prowess. Ted hit .406 the year Joe hit safely in 56 consecutive games. Both men were pitchers' nightmares: They hit for percentage and for distance.

There has been endless speculation over how their statistics might have differed had the two sluggers switched teams. DiMaggio, whom Williams considered the greatest right-handed hitter of all time, played in Yankee Stadium, which had a short right-field fence designed especially for Babe Ruth. The stadium was a paradise for left-handed hitters. Williams, who undoubtedly considered himself the greatest left-handed hitter of all time, played in Boston's Fenway Park, which had an inviting left-field fence for the benefit of right-handed pull hitters.

But the differences between the two sluggers went far beyond the difference between left and right.

DiMaggio was an easy-going fellow who enjoyed the approval of the crowd and the company of good companions. He was well known in New York cafe society and was idolized not only in Gotham but across the land.

Williams couldn't care less whether the fans at Fenway liked him. He was often booed by the home crowd. After hitting a home run, he would round third and head for the plate without tipping his hat to the fans. He didn't need their applause.

NOT FIT TO BE TIED

DiMaggio was a team player par excellence. Manager Joe McCarthy's dress code, requiring the Yankees to wear jackets and ties in public, even in hotel lobbies, was up Joe's alley. He represented Yankee dignity to the nth degree.

Williams was more the individualist, and he was an open-collared man to boot. The Red Sox had a similar jacket-and-tie dress code, but Ted hated ties and he stuck to his sport shirts. A minor Sox official, spotting Ted entering a hotel lobby in casual attire, warned him about the infraction.

Ted just glared at him and asked, "What am I hitting?" (Seidel, 1988, p. 35).

Ted's response showed indifference to the team image; C persons are not great team players. This illustrates another aspect of the C person. An I person might have responded like this: "Hey, what's wrong with this shirt? It's neat, it's clean, and it matches my slacks. It looks good on me. I don't see a thing wrong with wearing it in a hotel lobby." A D person would have said, "I've got a constitutional right to wear this shirt, and if you don't like it you can stuff it." An S person would have gone back to his room and put on a jacket and tie. But Williams didn't defend his attire. He simply cited his batting average. C persons tie their self-worth directly to their performance. They would subscribe to the philosophy of Deng Xiaoping, the pragmatic Chinese despot: "It doesn't matter what color a cat is, so long as it catches mice."

That was Williams' point: It doesn't matter what an outfielder wears as long as he's batting better than .300. Because performance is C people's principal measure of self-worth, when you criticize their performance you can be sure that they're taking it personally.

As an S person, DiMaggio took a somewhat more relaxed approach to perfecting his performance than Williams did. When Joe slumped, he reacted philosophically: "There is always a remedy. Time and confidence." If he kept swinging away in his usual style, eventually the hits would start falling in. Joe believed in the law of averages.

For Williams, more was involved. He wasn't content to wait for the odds to swing in his favor. A hit was not an accidental occurrence; it was a planned event.

PROCEDURE

"In order to do the toughest thing there is to do in sport — hit a baseball properly — a man has got to devote every ounce of concentration to it," Williams said (Seidel, 1988, p. 35). Note the C person's concern for quality. It isn't enough to hit the ball. One has to hit it "properly."

For DiMaggio, hitting was an art that he made into a form of poetry. For Williams, it was a science.

Babe Ruth, watching Williams hit in 1941, marveled at the quickness of his swing, which gave him a split second longer to read the pitch. Ruth had the mechanics right, concedes author Michael Seidel (1988), but he "wasn't privy yet, if he ever was, to Williams' elaborate theory of zoning the plate that made his selection of hittable pitches akin to Cartesian geometry" (p. 15).

C persons don't leave things to chance. They want to cover all bases and be prepared for all contingencies. Steady Hank Aaron was willing to isolate one pitch from a pitcher's repertoire and wait patiently for it to arrive. Ted Williams prepared for whatever came over the plate.

"No one could ever throw the ball past Williams anywhere in the strike zone," said Bob Feller, who could have done it if anybody could (Seidel, 1988, p. 15).

A Methodical Approach

Paterno showed a Williams-like cerebral approach when he looked for ways to solve his defensive problems after a mediocre 1966 season, his first as head coach. As Paterno (1989) put it, "I had to find a way of playing great defense without great defensive athletes." In the pattern of a C person, Paterno was not looking for quick fixes. He wanted a system that would work for the long pull.

The Cerebral Defense

During the summer of 1967, the coach retreated to a small hideaway upstairs in his home and went to work with pencil, paper and eraser. He eventually came up with the two-deep zone defense, which is commonly used today but was innovative back then. Paterno reasoned that if his seven-man defensive line was outmanned by the opposing team's offense, he might even the odds by putting an eighth man on the line. But that would mean robbing his backfield of a defender. Paterno solved this by borrowing an idea from the baseball outfield. When a ball is hit to the left, the center fielder shifts to back the left fielder and the right fielder covers center. Paterno would have his three defensive backs spread out and watch the quarterback.

> If he tried coming to our left on a sprint-out or option, our outside guy on that side would immediately come in to handle him. The middle man of the three, the safety, would shift to the left to back him. Then the third guy, from the far side, would shift over and play safety. (p. 96)

The Hypotenuse of the Secondary

Here's where the C person's cerebral prowess and passion for perfection came into play:

> After working out the principles of the plays, I had to figure lengths of hypotenuses between sides of triangles and whatnot to develop mathematical rules of where to place those men in the secondary. If the quarterback got the ball on the left hash, and if the guy you assume is the receiver is X yards from him and will be able to run 6 yards deep, I had to figure out just where my "left fielder" had to be, if he was of equal speed, to meet the intended receiver at 20 yards deep and prevent a completion. Then I figured out that the "center fielder" had to be as distant horizontally from the "left fielder" as the "left fielder" was down field from the potential receiver, and so forth. (Paterno, 1989, p. 99)

Talk about perfectionism! Nothing was left to chance. Positions were worked out with mathematical precision.

Paterno had his secondary mapped the way Williams mapped his strike zone.

Paterno here was demonstrating four strengths of the C person:

• He was analytical. He didn't put his feet on his desk, blow smoke rings and wait for inspiration. He analyzed the problem, and he used left-brain deductive reasoning to take him to a solution.

• He was disciplined. He had to be to spend all those hours alone with pen and paper in that upstairs hideaway when summer beckoned with so many pleasant things to do.

• He was thorough. He mentally tested each deployment scheme to make sure he had thought of every contingency.

• He was precise. It wasn't enough to estimate distances. He had to work them out with geometric precision.

Unlike D and I people, who may come up with great ideas that never get implemented, Paterno demonstrated the C person's capacity to follow through. When he introduced his concept to his coaching staff, he showed another C strength: orderliness. He did not spring the two-deep zone defense haphazardly. First, he sold the idea to his coaching staff. He had all his facts in hand, and he answered all their questions.

Paterno the perfectionist didn't leave it to others to implement his system. He personally taught it to his linebackers. He coached every position on defense until every member of his coaching staff understood the plan. "The best teacher," said Paterno (1989), "is not only the person who has the most knowledge, but the one who has his knowledge best organized and who knows how to state what he knows in different ways" (p. 102).

INFORMATIONAL ABSORPTION

C persons soak up information like sponges. They pick up on many complexities that others miss.

Joe McCarthy was such a person. He was known for

quietly sitting in the dugout, keeping an eye on everything that was going on and moving quickly to correct whatever wasn't right.

George Allen was another person who took meticulous note of what was happening around him. Paterno (1989) remembers the time when Allen, then coaching the Washington Redskins, came up to observe the Penn State coach during spring practice:

> As always, George showed up with a stenographer's note pad in his hand. "Why did you do this after that? Why'd you do that for only 10 minutes? Why do you keep the strength equipment at the end? How come you have that painted green?" And at times I'd have to answer, "There may have been a reason, but I can't remember it." And he kept taking notes, notes, notes. (p. 128)

Like their fellow introverts, the S people, Cs dislike conflict. You seldom see them haranguing an umpire. In fact, when bickering breaks out, C people tend to absent themselves. Yelling at officials and losing control of yourself are practices incompatible with excellence, Paterno (1989) maintains.

Joe McCarthy seldom quarreled with umpires. Once, while managing the Yankees, he was thrown out of a game for expressing himself too forcefully to an arbiter. The experience was so rare that McCarthy didn't even know he was supposed to leave the park. He returned to the bench and continued to manage. The umpire had to notify him that unless he left he would be fined.

Sixteen years later another umpire ended a discussion by barking "Get out of here" at McCarthy. Joe, remembering the previous episode, headed for the locker room. He didn't realize that the umpire meant only for him to go back to the dugout.

Wrote Ed Fitzgerald (1973):

> He prefers to sit in majestic silence on the bench. Joe being a man who figures all the percentages right down to the last decimal point, the chances are good that he thinks the umpires know when they have booted one and

can be relied on to square things at the earliest opportunity. (p. 248)

STRUCTURE

Another characteristic of C people is their insistence on doing things "the right way," which, of course, is their way.

I learned this shortly after marrying a person who was a High C: The honeymoon was barely over and we had settled into our small house. I had just done the laundry for the first time. As an I person, I expected my husband to be full of compliments for my tidiness.

Instead, I heard a horrified exclamation coming from the bedroom.

What was wrong? His sock drawer, which I thought was so neat and orderly, was in a state of anarchy. Didn't I know that his socks should be arranged alphabetically, according to color?

He was really serious about it, though not serious enough to make it the litmus issue in our marriage. After we had made up, I told him how I wanted him to arrange my things when he did the laundry: Just open the drawer, stand in the door and pitch 'em in. That's the I way.

Brides have certain advantages over athletic coaches. If you're not in the honeymoon mode, don't expect a C person to acknowledge that your way is right unless you can produce the documenting facts.

Sometimes it takes the gentle intervention of a third party to swing stubborn Cs around. Rip Engle, Paterno's mentor at Brown and at Penn State, seems to have exerted a moderating influence on Paterno's C tendencies.

During Paterno's first season as head coach, when he was pushing his team too hard, he remembered Engle's admonition: "Always remember: This is their team, not yours." He also recalled his father's recurring question: "Did you have any fun?" (Paterno, 1989, pp. 94-95).

Too Much Perfection

It's C people's passion for perfection that often trips them in coaching. Billy Martin observed, "As a rule, great players don't make good managers. The reason is that superstars seem to lack the patience to accept mediocrity in their players and, let's face it, the majority of your players are going to be average or mediocre."

Martin could have substituted "C persons" for "superstars." He maintained that Ted Williams proved the point: "Great hitter. Great hitting instructor. Lousy manager. In four seasons, his teams never finished higher than fourth" (Martin, 1987, pp. 14-15).

Martin also faulted Gene Mauch for being "too smart":

> To me, he's the classic case of the guy who overmanages. He tries to be so brilliant. He takes the game away from his players. His problem is that he often tries to show how much he knows, how much more he knows about the game than the guy in the other dugout, and it often backfires on him....[T]he game is not as complicated as he makes it. (Martin, 1987, p. 34)

Leo Durocher had a similar opinion of Mauch: "Stick with that little genius and you'll stay in last place" (Bouton, 1973, p. 197).

Jim Bouton (1973b, p. xix) illustrates the pitfalls of the C-style manager by comparing Harry Walker with Ralph Houk, who exhibited I characteristics:

> The best field manager I ever played for—the best strategist, the most knowledgeable, the most observant, the most thorough, the most daring manager I ever played for — was Harry Walker. But...Walker simply could not get players to play well for him the way Houk could. Even though Harry knew more about baseball, Houk new more about baseball players. The ballplayers, particularly the older players, didn't like Harry because he was constantly pointing out what they were doing wrong or reminding them of what they should be doing.
>
> We'd be lounging in the Astro bullpen and Harry would call down to tell us to be alert so we could holler to our right fielder which base to throw to in the event he had to turn his back to get a ball off the wall. An important detail that could mean the ball game, and only Harry Walker would think of it. Then we'd spend the rest of the

game griping about what a pain Harry Walker was to interfere with our leisure time. (p. xix)

Reaches and Grasps

Paterno was smart enough to rein in his perfectionist tendencies, perhaps remembering Engle's easygoing example.

During his first year as head coach, "I had worked the team hard in practice, pushing them to reach for their limits, even beyond, with absolute concentration on football." He believed in the sentiments expressed by Robert Browning: "Ah, but a man's reach should exceed his grasp, or what's a heaven for?" (Joe debunks the old theory that coaches and athletes can't be literate.)

But Paterno came to realize that "I must have driven those kids to reach too far beyond their grasp. The squad began muttering behind my back so loud I couldn't help but hear. They had played well under Rip Engle, who had formed them, and had played well for me as Rip's assistant. Now they were unhappy with their overeager new coach" (Paterno, 1989, p. 93).

Faced with a maiden season that early on looked like a loser, says Paterno (1989):

> I loosened up a little, not going for the last turn of the screw, not forgetting to sprinkle on a little kidding and joking and, especially, deserved praise. Something relaxed and lightened. We did lose two more games that season, to Syracuse and Georgia Tech, but lifted ourselves to break even, at 5-5. More important, we became a smarter group of people, coached by a more sensitive newcomer. (p. 95)

As Paterno (1989) observed, "The other side of being a good teacher is sensing when to get off their backs, when to say, 'Let's knock off today and have some laughs, and tomorrow we'll start all over again—from a higher plateau'" (p. 83).

LOOSENING UP

Rigidity is another pitfall for the C coach to beware. Some C coaches try to arrange their line-ups scientifically so that each player fits in the niche where the individual can make the greatest contribution toward victory. But Robert Burns' adage about the best laid plans of men and mice keeps applying. The ideal quarterback may come down with the flu. The left-handed fast-baller who is most effective against the visiting sluggers may develop a sore arm. The fast runner you'd counted on for the final leg of the relay may develop a blister on her heel. The C coach has to develop flexibility.

C people are not interactors. They don't stand around water coolers talking to their associates the way an I person might. They like to stay to themselves; they value their privacy. It isn't that they're anti-social. It's just that their behavior style is more oriented toward tasks than toward people.

Like their fellow introverts, the Ss, they are likely to keep their opinions bottled up. They may be critical about the way their peers are performing a task, but they will share their thoughts only on a need-to-know basis. The C person doesn't go in for small talk.

S persons care what you think; they want you to like them. I persons also care what you think; they want you to admire and even envy them. C persons are not so concerned with what you think. They are driven by the demands of their internal standards, not by the need for external approval. Therefore, C persons may not go to a great deal of trouble to get along with people they dislike. Ted Williams didn't go out of his way to make enemies. But he wouldn't put on a jacket and tie just to make a friend.

Yet C people need feedback from their associates. Joe Paterno benefited from knowing what his players were saying behind his back. It enabled him to make the adjustments in coaching style that turned the Nittany Lions back into winners.

FACING IMPERFECTION

C persons know they're imperfect, but they keep looking for evidence that they're not. They will even manipulate information to prove that they're right, and they become angry and depressed if they're proven wrong.

Often, when trying something new, they will avoid people

who they think might criticize what they're doing. This sometimes results in communications breakdowns. If they think the boss is likely to say "no" to a project, they'll go ahead with the project on the sly. Some people might call that being sneaky.

C people are hesitant to try totally new approaches. They have studied the way things work and they know what has worked in the past. They like proven dependability. However, a C person may take a system that works and try to modify or perfect it into a new, improved version.

C persons thrive best on tasks that are oriented to detail. If you need someone to audit the books, turn to a C. C people work best when they have a clear understanding of what's expected of them and when they're given plenty of time for planning.

Critical Reaction

It bears repeating that C people take criticism personally because they identify their worth so closely with their performance. That doesn't mean that the coach should never criticize C athletes. There's a way to go about it: First compliment them. Then take up the things you want them to change.

Remember that C persons are suspicious of change. Change throws in variables that open up opportunities for error. If changes have to be made, give your C people plenty of advance notice. Give them a chance to explore the consequences of the change and to plot strategy for dealing with them.

C people need a lot of explanation and a lot of information. What they don't appreciate is a lot of bull. When talking to them, remember what Ed Fitzgerald (1973) said of Joe McCarthy: "What he had to say was always short, stripped of unnecessary wordage, and to the point" (p. 246).

When you're trying to teach Cs something, start with the most important points. Then demonstrate what you want them to do, as logically as you know how. With each step, explain to the athlete why it's done that way. Take it slower than you would take it with a D or an I, and stop often to make sure the athlete understands you. You may even want to ask for suggestions about how the process can be improved.

C persons will ask questions for clarification. What they need from you are many details and lots of reassurance, especially if you're trying to correct something they're doing wrong. And they'll demand documentation.

Data and Corroboration

Pat Riley once went to great lengths to assemble a collection of edited videotapes showing Kareem Abdul-Jabbar where he needed to improve on the basketball court. When it was over, Jabbar told him:

> Whatever you want. But the next time we meet like this, I would rather have to respond to more objective analysis — not just visual. Pat, this is strictly visual and subjective. All you did was pick out the bad things. It's an arbitrary analysis of me not doing well in isolated parts of these games. Now, I don't resent it. I understand where you're coming from and I'll do my best to supply you with that. But I want you to supply me with statistical data to corroborate what you've said. (Riley, 1988, p. 233)

When C players ask questions, the coach should not become defensive. Give them straight, simple answers in a non-threatening manner.

EXCELLENCE VS. PERFECTION

C persons have unrealistic expectations that frequently cause them to feel sorry for themselves.

Diana Nyad (1978) describes what it's like for a C person to face the possibility of falling short in a cherished undertaking:

> Fear comes quickly on the heels of self-doubt. Fear that I am not worthy of the goal, that the commitment has been too heavy, that I have risked showing myself a quitter by chasing such an unreasonable dream. (p. 10)

Diana felt like a quitter when she had to give up on an attempt to swim across the English Channel. Sickened by the choppy waters and unable to keep down the chocolate drink she took for nourishment, she collapsed and had to be dragged from the water. Later, she recalled her feelings: "I had failed, given up. I had been weak; I hadn't been disciplined enough to make myself do it just because I said I could and I would. I felt somehow guilty." But she would try again: "It was not the pure desire to win, to finish; it was more the loathing of the self-respect I would lose if I quit" (Nyad, 1978, p. 132).

The discerning coach will help C athletes see the difference between excellence and perfection. The first is a worthy, and achievable, goal. The second is beyond human reach, and those who make it their unalterable aim can wreck their careers and destroy themselves in the bargain.

6

Chemistry in Action

We've looked at the four core styles of behavior, with some brief glimpses of the classical behavior patterns. We've seen how various sports figures have exemplified the traits of the core styles. We've also seen how different combinations work out in the coaching environment. And we've reviewed some tips on dealing with the various styles of behavior in athletes and in staff members.

Now let's look at how the behavior styles work together on the field and in the gym.

The smart coach knows that it isn't enough to produce a physically fit team. Joe Paterno (1989) put it this way:

> Football is played, above all, with the heart and mind. It's played with the body only secondarily. A coach's first duty is to coach minds. If he doesn't succeed at that, his team will not reach its potential. (p. 81)

GENERATING THE CORE CHEMISTRY

To "coach the mind," one must be able to recognize the behavior styles through which the mind perceives the world and responds to it. A compatible combination of behavior styles can mean the difference between a smooth-functioning winning team and a discordant, though talented, losing team.

The Lakers' Pat Riley (1988) realized the importance of putting together talents in the right combination.

"You see, a great team isn't simply built by hiring the top talent," he said. "Just as in any other form of business, it also matters how those top talents combine with each other."

Riley remembers the year the Lakers acquired James Worthy. He picked Worthy because "his attributes synchronize with those of our other stars." Observed Riley:

> It's no accident that we selected James first in a draft year that also offered a choice of Dominique Wilkins, who led the league in scoring through '85-86, and Terry Cummings, who was subsequently named rookie of the year. Those two are undeniably great players, but James fits better than either of them into the Laker style of basketball. That's what is called chemistry. Attitude and chemistry are factors that can kick people up to higher levels of winning, no matter what talent they have." (p. 41)

Staying Worthy

Now let's look at how the Laker management's shrewd reading of behavior styles helped keep Worthy on the team and helped him mesh well with his more colorful teammates.

After the disappointment of 1986, owner Jerry Buss was ready to trade Worthy for Mark Aguirre of the Dallas Mavericks. Buss wanted a big man to pry the defenses off the aging Kareem Abdul-Jabbar. But General Manager Jerry West saw beyond the physical attributes. He knew that the core of the Lakers was sound and the chemistry was good. Worthy was a nice complement to Earvin "Magic" Johnson.

"Earvin can push the ball upcourt at an incredible tempo, but he needs someone even faster than himself to break for the wing and fly upcourt," observed Riley.

West also worried about Aguirre's history of trouble with the Mavericks' coach, Dick Motta. Perhaps he remembered the problems created when the flashy Johnson joined the team and took the spotlight off the proud and aggressive Norm Nixon. Nixon's inability to adjust to his new status caused management to replace him with Byron Scott. West decided to stick with Worthy, even though Buss had wanted Aguirre.

News of the possible trade had reached Worthy, however, and Worthy had become suspicious. Aguirre and Johnson had the same agent. Worthy suspected that Johnson might have been trying to get him off the team.

Worthy follows a behavior style quite different from that of the flashy, life-of-the-party Magic Johnson.

As Riley put it:

> Where one is gregarious and always ready to joke and create a loose atmosphere, the other values his dignity and is more of a solitary presence. It wasn't hard for James to think out a connection like this: "Earvin is in tight with the owner. I was never a rah-rah guy, but I always did my job. Now they think they'll be better off without me." (Riley, 1988, p. 41)

The situation could have created the same kind of unhappiness that caused Nixon to be dropped from the team. But Worthy's problem was not an ego that needed to be fed. It was the S person's need for affirmation — the need to know he was appreciated.

Fortunately, Magic Johnson recognized that his quiet teammate was not a competing ego but a potential ally on and off the court. He used his outgoing charm to establish a link with Worthy. During the summer, the two men got together and achieved what Riley described as a "breakthrough":

> The trade rumor stuff got put away and now I think the two are far more accepting of each other's differences. You won't likely see James at a disco or at a tailor shop ordering a custom leather suit, and you won't see Earvin headed to a relatively modest home in a used Toyota either. But they don't pass judgment on each other's lifestyle. (Riley, 1988, pp. 41-42)

With James Worthy and with Michael Cooper, Riley recognized the appropriate way of dealing with an S person. We have already seen how Riley headed off Cooper's thoughts about leaving the team and becoming a free agent because of difficulties in negotiations. Riley played on Cooper's natural loyalty as an S person, his family ties to Los Angeles, his comfort level among friendly teammates who liked him, and his instinctive fear of the unknown: What if he jumped to a new team and found the atmosphere uncongenial?

Motivating Mantle

Casey Stengel and Ralph Houk relied on different characteristics of the S person to get the most out of Mickey Mantle.

Stengel, an I person when dealing with the press, was apparently a D while managing the team. With Mantle in particular he seemed to be cool and unfeeling. Instinctively, he knew that Mantle took pride in his performance, had a basic feeling of inadequacy and would go to great lengths to conceal that inadequacy. Casey knew that Mantle's ailing legs sometimes left him in agony. Instead of being solicitous about his star outfielder's condition, Stengel took the attitude that if Mantle wanted to sit out a game he should come forward and say so.

When S people hurt, they either try harder or they withdraw. Mantle didn't withdraw. He made it a point of honor to play even when he was hurting.

Ralph Houk, as a manager, was a more sensitive I. As Edward Linn (1973) noted:

> It was no accident that when Ralph Houk took over, he immediately appointed Mantle captain and held forth whenever possible on Mickey's value to the team. (p. 70)

Houk recognized his S star's yearning for affirmation, his need for assurance that he was liked and appreciated.

ENCOURAGING S ASSERTIVENESS

S people need constant assurance that they're liked. But because they are passive, they also need to be encouraged to assert themselves. Their placid demeanors may hide a lot of inner turmoil. They may feel inadequate and be afraid their weaknesses will be exposed. So long as there's no tension, they feel safe. But when conflict arises, they see the possibility that their shortcomings will surface. When they shun conflict, it's not because they don't have strong feelings. They're just turning those feelings inward.

A coach needs to work hard to develop friendships with S athletes. This will help the coach discern when things are troubling the player. S athletes need to be encouraged to confront others when they're angry and the occasion calls for it.

Particularly when things aren't going well, they need to be assured of continuing affection and high regard, regardless of how poorly they're doing in competition. Only when they have that assurance can they respond with full-bore performance.

Bobby Knight provides the example in his approach to Michael Jordan when Jordan was playing below par while practicing for the 1984 Olympics. As Knight recalled it:

> I walked up to him and I grabbed him by the arm, and I just squeezed his arm. I'd say, "You're too damned good to play like this." And Jordan looked me in the eye and said, "You're right," and he'd play better. (Mellen, 1988-89, p. 23)

It wasn't Knight's style to ladle out the flattery. But he did let Jordan know that he respected his ability while urging him to improve on his performance.

USING I TO MOTIVATE

We have seen how Pat Riley used Magic Johnson, his premier I player, to soothe the feelings of S star James Worthy. Ed Temple found an I athlete useful too in motivating a talented S runner.

Mae Faggs, recalls Temple (1980), "was one more stick of dynamite. She also had the experience and poise, and she willingly passed it on to the others." The I Faggs particularly related to the younger, quieter Wilma (Skeeter) Rudolph. Faggs and Rudolph made a Mutt-and-Jeff combination: Mae stood 5 feet 2 and Wilma stood 6 feet.

Faggs was the first American woman to participate in three Olympics. She also was the first Tennessee State athlete to win a Pan-American gold medal and the second to be inducted into the National Track and Field Hall of Fame. "She wasn't the first on the team, not the fastest and not the best, but without her TSU and the Tigerbelles might not be on the map," wrote Temple (1980, p. 61).

He remembers particularly how she motivated the 14-year-old Rudolph to excel when he took his Tigerbelles to Washington, D. C., for the Olympic trials:

> The United States was sending the top three in each event to the Olympics. In the 100, Faggs had placed first, [Isabelle] Daniels second and [Lucinda] Williams third. Willye B. [White] and Margaret [Matthews] had gotten first and second in the long jump, so we had already placed five on the team. The 220 was near the end and Rudolph hadn't made the team as yet. So Faggs, being the older, motherly type, told her, "Now look, Skeeter, if you're gonna make this boat I'm going to tell you what to do. When that gun cracks, I want you to lay right on my shoulder. If you stay right on my shoulder, you can make this team...." Rudolph pulled up beside Faggs, and Mae was just churning those little legs. Being experienced, Faggs won by leaning at the tape, because at that time Rudolph didn't know anything about leaning at any tape. Faggs barely got first, Rudolph second and Lucinda third. Faggs jogged on down the track about 15 yards, came back and put her hands on her hips. She looked up at Rudolph and said, "Now look. I told you to stay on my shoulder. I didn't tell you to go and act no fool and try to pass me." (Temple, 1980, pp. 62-63)

Wilma later became the first woman athlete to win three gold medals in the Olympics, and she joined Faggs in the Hall of Fame.

The Winning Spirit

Your I players can provide the spark that puts the winning spirit into your team. Riley (1988) observed the difference when Earvin "Magic" Johnson was out of the line-up.

With Johnson out, "Michael Cooper got his chance to run the offense. He piled up very good numbers and we won both games, 96-93 and 99-91. But it was obvious we were missing Earvin. Michael can run the offense just as well as Earvin, when it comes to calling plays and getting the ball to the right people. But when it comes to beating pressure defenses, Earvin can create unlike anyone else. Stress time, for Earvin, is simply opportunity time" (pp. 159-160).

This relish for the limelight can give the coach a means of motivating the I athlete. Mary Lou Retton came into her own as a gymnast only after she was given an opportunity to shine in practice.

"Mary Lou was an ambitious kid, and when people were doing better than she was, I could see the determination in her eyes," said her trainer, Bela Karolyi (Retton and Karolyi, 1986, p. 90).

Impatient

Mary Lou was an impatient I, and it was hard for her to follow the repetitive routine necessary to get consistency into her performance. Karolyi found a way to motivate her: He had her practice alongside Dianne Durham.

"Dianne was the main obstacle to her being the best athlete in our program, and it set up an unbelievable competitive situation," said Karolyi (Retton and Karolyi, 1986, p. 91).

Recalls Retton:

> When you see your teammate doing well, you want to do even better, and it just keeps going. It even happens in practice. Someone goes up and does a trick and you want to improve on it. It's like you have judges every day. (Retton and Karolyi, 1986, p. 84)

As she recounts, the competition stimulated Mary Lou in practice and it spurred her to stellar performance when medals were at stake:

> I can't say I like having pressure on me. I don't think anybody does. But somehow it brings out the best in me. There's always that nervous feeling, that twinge in your stomach, and I don't know if it means I'm anxious or just ready to go. But I think it's something that every competitor has, and I need that. (Retton and Karolyi, 1986, p. 99)

When Karolyi was training Nadia Comaneci in Romania, he was at pains to keep the media away, to keep the stress of the limelight from disturbing his privacy-loving star. Whether it was the more open American environment or an instinct for an I star's needs, Karolyi let Retton sparkle in the press.

After her triumphant 1983 performance in the McDonald's American Cup in New York City, Mary Lou remembers, "I wound up on the cover of the next issue of International Gymnast, which was a big deal with me. After that, I could sense other girls looking at me, watching me warm up, and saying, 'She's the one who won the American Cup. She beat Yurchenko and Agache and McNamara and everybody' " (Retton and Karolyi, 1986, p. 100).

The Passion to Score

This taste for the limelight imbues I athletes with the passion to score. The coach may have to put some extra effort into teaching them to be aggressive defenders.

Pat Riley (1988) found this to be true in the case of Byron Scott:

> If he didn't get good offensive numbers, he assumed everyone was down on him. He would lose concentration on defense. From three consecutive misses on 18- to 20-foot jump shots, his whole game would begin to drift. When I would bring in a reserve for him it would be almost like a penance. I don't want him thinking like that. I have confidence in him. I know he's going to get nothing but better. (p. 71)

Let us make a parenthetical note here of the I person's fear of public embarrassment. When Riley sent in a reserve for Scott, the athlete felt as if he were being publicly faulted, and that was a motivational downer. It's best, when possible, to wait a decent interval after a bad play before relieving an I athlete. Or better yet, send in the reliever before fatigue or other factors set the I person up for a fall.

But Riley's challenge was somehow to convince Scott that his value to the team didn't depend totally on his offensive prowess. That realization seems to have come during a game with the New York Knicks, when Scott and Worthy both got off to flying starts offensively. The offensive success gave Byron a new pride in his defensive performance.

"Byron came into his own as a defensive force in that game," said Riley. "Every time there was an opportunity to fill the gap in the lane, to help someone who had shifted position, he did it."

"I've taken more pride in my defense this year," Scott told reporters after the game (Riley, 1988, p. 71).

Some coaches may motivate I athletes on defense by telling them, "You're not going to get a chance at offense until you get your defensive act together." Others may find it effective to give defensive standouts warm public recognition. Find a way to put glory into the defense and you've found a way to motivate your I athlete to seek defensive excellence. Some coaches have done this by creating colorful names for defensive units. Louisiana State's "Chinese Bandits," the University of Georgia's "Junkyard Dogs" and the Washington Redskins' "Hogs" come to mind.

The Tendency to Oversell

The thing to watch in I athletes is a tendency to oversell their abilities. They sometimes acquire a confidence in their skills before they have mastered them. The coach may have to discourage them from showing off in a game with fancy new moves that need to be perfected first in practice.

Bobby Knight made clever use of this tendency to exceed the skill level when the Big Ten inaugurated the three-point rule. Knight let it be known that only three players in the conference were capable of making three-pointers and that two of them played for the University of Indiana. He refused to name the third (Mellen, 1989, p. 24).

Thereafter, Indiana benefited from a succession of opposing players who each tried to prove — unsuccessfully — that he was the third person. One can only speculate that the majority of those players who were shooting beyond their range were I people while the rest, no doubt, were Ds. Knight called it one of the best defensive moves he ever made.

PUTTING D IN DRIVE

The dominant D athlete can be the team sparkplug, particularly if the drive to dominate is accompanied by athletic talent.

Sometimes the drive to excel compensates for a lack of talent. Billy Martin, Eddy Stanky and Leo Durocher are examples of athletes who were not abundantly blessed with raw ability. But they had an aggressive determination that made things happen on the field; that kept their teams in competition even when the hits weren't coming or the grounders were taking bad hops.

The coach's challenge with D players is to teach them the value of teamwork and to make sure their aggressiveness doesn't intimidate others on the team.

The Pain of Losing

D athletes experience real pain when they lose. Their aggressiveness stems from a desire to avoid that pain at all costs. They may feel that way because their parents always praised them when they succeeded, but said nothing when they did poorly. If so, they grew up believing that their self-worth was tied directly to their performance. To lose meant to suffer rejection. Hence, losing became particularly painful.

D persons will pursue their zeal for winning regardless of how it makes others feel. If you appeal to their compassion, they'll think you're going soft. They are results-oriented.

The Hunger to Win

Billy Martin (1987) just couldn't understand how his non-D athletes could take losing so lightly:

> They'll come in after a game with their dirty hands and go right to the food table. They can't wait to get to that damn food. Even after losing the toughest game in the world, the first thing they do is go right to the food table. And your coaches are right there along with them. That kills me. My stomach is in such knots after a tough loss that I couldn't even get any food down. I'd probably throw it right up if I did. But these guys are eating like

the Russians are marching down Broadway.... Then, boom, they're showered and they're gone, and you're sitting there saying, "What am I knocking myself out for? These guys don't even care. They don't care whether they win or lose." (pp. 151-152)

What Martin didn't understand was that these people didn't enjoy losing, either. But they had other sources of self-esteem. They didn't believe that losing made them somehow unworthy.

The Best Medicine

D athletes may need some instruction in listening to others and identifying with their concerns. The coach can help by establishing a friendly environment when dealing with the team.

D athletes need to be commended whether they win or lose. They need to know that winning, however nice, really isn't everything; nor is it the only thing.

But since winning is nearly always better than losing, we need to help the D athlete win. If the coach can convince his D quarterback that throwing the ball to the other guy can help the team win, if she can convince her aggressive forward that passing the ball to her unguarded teammate nearer the basket is the best way to score a goal and put the team ahead, then the D's passion for victory will help the whole team.

Sometimes your D people's headstrong instincts must be indulged so they can experience the consequences of bad decisions or negative conflict and learn from the experience. Often, though, the D just needs a sounding board — someone with an understanding ear who can let the restless D get things off his or her chest. An easygoing S can be the catalyst here.

Confrontation

Still, it's sometimes necessary to confront Ds directly. But when you confront them, focus on their actions, not on their character and integrity. Don't beat around the bush. Get to the point and make it clear to them that the conduct you disapprove of will not be tolerated.

Temple Takes No Foolishness

Ed Temple was direct and decisive with Willye B. White, one of his most promising runners.

"After one quarter of foolishness," he said, "I told her, 'Somebody's got to go, Red, and I've been here a long time so I don't plan to go.'" (Temple called her "Red" because you never knew what color her hair would be from one day to the next.) It was a tough decision, but Temple made it stick.

"Since that time," he wrote, "Red and I have worked on teams overseas, and she cooperates with me 100%. We are the greatest of friends. But until this day, she'll tell any young ones who are interested in coming to Tennessee State — and she'll tell them quick — 'Now you can go down there if you want to, but he ain't having no mess'" (Temple, 1980, p. 49).

Paterno Gets Tough

Joe Paterno faced a similar situation in 1967 after a game with the University of Miami in Florida. As he strolled through the air terminal waiting to board the team's charter flight, he saw two of his best players standing in the airport bar drinking beer, in violation of a clearly stated team rule. They knew the coach had seen them. One of the players had been in minor trouble with the police before.

"You're gone," Paterno told that player, permanently ejecting him from the team. To the other he said, "This is the first trouble I know about. You get one more chance, but you're suspended for the next two games."

Later, the players held a meeting and sent word through the team captains that they felt the penalties were too harsh. They wanted the captains to return to the meeting with Paterno's answer. Paterno took the answer back himself: "A rule that protects us all was broken," he said. "The decision I made was the best one for all of us. I have no choice but to stand with it. If anybody here can't live with it, go. Right now. If you stay, you do it my way, the right way, living by the rules. If you decide to stay and do it that way, we'll have a great football team. I'm going to walk out of here right now. A minute later I'm coming back in. Whoever's here, that's who we're going to play with."

Nobody left.

Paterno records with pride that both the disciplined players went on to become successes — one as a veterinarian, the other as an NFL player for five years, then as a stockbroker (Paterno, 1989, pp. 114-117).

The D zeal for success can be channeled in a positive way. When you want a D to do something, put it in the form of a challenge. Ds find challenges hard to resist. They'll persist until they're rewarded with success.

"CHEERING" C EFFECTIVELY

If all athletes were Cs and Ds there would be no need for cheerleaders. The D athlete has an inner need to succeed that requires no egging on from the sidelines. The C athlete steers by an inner compass that does not respond to applause but stays steadily fixed in one direction: toward perfection.

Help Make the Work Pay Off

Hence, all the coach's locker-room eloquence is likely to be lost on C players. You don't need to tell them how good they are; they've already figured that out in a quite logical way. You don't need to tell them to fight! fight! fight! for dear old Alma Mater. They're fighting for something that transcends old school ties. They're searching for the perfect moment in performance—the supreme achievement.

Nyad's Quest

"I learned that long-distance swims are recorded throughout the years as homage to that notion that man with his insignificant size and strength can occasionally affirm his place and his power in the universe by defying and conquering the elements," wrote Diana Nyad.

It is this striving toward a goal that is larger than life that keeps the C person competing. As Nyad observed later:

> I realize at the end of all circuit races that the pride I enjoy is in victory over the elements; the reason the marathon racers are so close for the most part is that

they share that same victory over the elements even more than they relish the minor victories over each other. (Nyad, 1978, p. 22)

It is this devotion to perfection that makes C athletes willing to devote hours to practice, practice, practice, learning what works best and how best to do it.

Nadia's Triumph

It's this devotion Bela Karolyi saw in Nadia Comaneci. The bubbly Mary Lou Retton, however, wanted to flit from one task to another and bored quickly of the repetitive tasks necessary to achieve consistency. Not Nadia. According to Karolyi:

> Nadia was an unbelievably hard worker. She was strong-willed and 100% dedicated. If Nadia was sick she wouldn't even pay attention to it. She would have a high fever all week and we'd never find out. Her mother would have to tell us, because we could never see it in her performance in the gym. People said she had no emotions at all. And it is true that Nadia's basic personality wasn't too open....But she was a hard-working, determined, excellent athlete. (Retton and Karolyi, 1986, p. 40)

Karolyi takes us back to the time of the 1976 Montreal Olympics, scene of Nadia's triumph:

> The public and the media are pushing you up into seventh heaven. But Nadia is able to ignore all this and put together a fantastic performance. (Retton and Karolyi, 1986, p. 41)

Note that Mary Lou drew energy from the spotlight, but for Nadia the pageantry was something to be put out of mind. Applause is not the energizer for the perfectionist C. And while Mary Lou was fired up by competing with others in the Karolyi gym, Nadia, as Karolyi indicates, was fired by the passion for excellence:

> I didn't try to change her personality, because at that time I think it could have been a mistake and ended up

a big mess. My mentality and hers was very much the same: Go and make it. Go and do it. Don't joke around. Forget everything else. Take 100% seriously your job; that is what you have been working for. (Retton and Karolyi, 1986, p. 40)

The result for Nadia was a one-of-a-kind performance. She won five medals: three gold, one silver and one bronze. But even beyond that, she compiled seven perfect scores.

It wasn't the rah-rahs that vaulted Nadia to acclaim. It was the hard work, the total dedication to perfection. If you want to help C athletes, don't bore them with pep talks. Tell them how to do their jobs more perfectly. Give them pointers on technique. And be prepared to document what you say.

Be Ready to Document

Even the documentation of a video camera wasn't enough for Kareem Abdul-Jabbar when Pat Riley wanted to help his superstar improve his game. Kareem demanded statistical corroboration, and Riley put together a system that would oblige him. Wrote Riley (1988):

> Thus were born the rebound effort charts, shot chart analysis, plus and minus ratings to show them exactly and irrefutably what their production numbers are — just as salespeople always see where they stand, relative to the averages for their district, relative to the other producers in the office. Just as the Goodyear plant knows how many radial tires they've got to turn out in an eight-hour shift. (p. 233)

That's language the C athlete understands.

C athletes are the most likely to become students of the game, accumulating an encyclopedic knowledge of their own craft and of the weaknesses of the opposition. Honus Wagner, the great Pittsburgh shortstop, studied the habits of other players. When the grounder seemed to make straight for the Flying Dutchman's glove, it was no fluke of luck. Wagner knew the hitter's pattern and was usually waiting in the right place (Thorn, 1976, p. 44-45).

Such knowledge could be invaluable to C's coach and teammates if C would only share it. But C persons are introverts and are not prone to idle chatter. If they spot a flaw in a teammate's execution, they aren't likely to go to the teammate or the coach to point out the flaw. C people won't give opinions unless they're asked. But if you do ask, you may find that they expect far more of themselves — and of others — than can reasonably be delivered.

These high expectations lead C persons to be cautious. No one is perfect, and they know that. So rather than fall below the standards of perfection, they may withdraw from the attempt. Where there are no risks, there are no failures. The C person hesitates to take chances until all the information is in.

D Paterno vs. C Paterno

Note how the D and the C sides of Joe Paterno struggled with each other in a game against Bear Bryant's Alabama Crimson Tide.

It was New Year's Day, 1979, at the Sugar Bowl in New Orleans. The winners would be the undisputed national champions. With less than two minutes remaining in the game, Penn State trailed 14-7. It was fourth and goal for the Nittany Lions inside the 'Bama one-yard line. A touchdown and a two-pointer would give Paterno's team the championship.

Years later, Paterno could still feel the victory in his grasp:

> What a perfect moment. There, steeled against us, the great Red Tide. And we — We are Penn State! — perennial winners, until now never the acknowledged champs. There was Bear Bryant.
>
> Here was Joe Paterno. In this play I go hand to hand, my destined chance to outcoach a legend.

Pass or Run?

Joe wanted to call a fake run and let his quarterback, Chuck Fusina, throw a little pop pass to the tight end.

"I didn't doubt that experienced, poised Chuck would handle it perfectly."

Paterno's assistants advised him to play the percentages and let tailback Mike Guman — a fine leaper — hurdle across a couple of feet for the score.

"If we can't do this and score a yard," one of them said, "we don't deserve a national championship."

"With an eerie clarity," wrote Paterno, "I still remember the sure voice of my instinct: 'That's a lot of crap. This is the time to surprise them and throw the football.'" That was his D style speaking.

Then the Paterno C piped up: "Hold it, Joe. What if..."

"That moment," wrote the coach, "was one of the few in my life when I backed off from a strong instinct and let myself worry about what people might say if a decision was wrong. Especially what the coaching staff would say if they turned out right and I turned out wrong."

Guman took the ball and leaped for the goal.

"To this day, down in Alabama, anywhere you go you can find their blown-up photo: an army of Crimson defenders stopping Guman cold," Paterno laments.

Revenge

Paterno's D got its revenge four years later in the same bowl against another Southeastern Conference team — and again with a national championship at stake. Penn State was up against Herschel Walker and the University of Georgia. The Bulldogs had rallied from a 10-point half-time deficit and trailed 27-23 with 1:37 on the clock. The Nittany Lions held the ball, 3rd and 3, in their own territory. If they didn't get the first down, they would have to punt. A punt would give Georgia an opportunity to score and win. Penn State had to keep possession.

The assistant coaches said, "Run the ball. We can't afford an interception."

Quarterback Todd Blackledge said, "I think we can throw it for a first down."

"My gut believed him," said Paterno.

But his C voice again piped up: "No, no. Play the percentages and run."

"Throw it," said Paterno, letting his D take charge.

Blackledge threw. Gregg Garrity grabbed the pass, and in so doing grabbed the game and the national championship for Penn State (Paterno, 1989, pp. 214-215).

When it comes to mastering technique, developing strategy, and executing flawlessly, the C athlete will excel. When the need is for decisiveness and risk-taking, go with your D. When the spotlight is on, the air is electric and the moment of glory is at hand, search your line-up for that "thunderclap waiting for the moment" — your dashing I person. When the team is antsy, nerves are taut and the need is for someone to calm the herd, call on steady, dependable S.

Know your players and their behavior styles. Just as important, know yourself and your coaches. And when the chips are down, know which of your behavior styles is right for the moment.

7

Non-Verbal Cues

The winning spirit is not something that can be put on with a uniform or absorbed from the atmosphere of a gym or stadium. It's something the coach has to communicate to the team.

EXPECTATIONS

That doesn't necessarily mean that the victory goes to the coach with the most eloquent tongue. Often the most effective communication is not the verbal kind, but the messages conveyed by a coach's bearing and posture.

As Joe Paterno (1989) observed:

> When Bear Bryant... walked out on that football field, self-confidence hung in the air around him like a fine mist. That was worth at least one touchdown for Alabama. Confidence was the secret ingredient of Bryant's greatness and of Lombardi's legend. (p. 82)

Mike Hebert, volleyball coach at the University of Illinois, would agree. Hebert once asked a former player what made the biggest difference in her desire to win. The answer: "The fact that you acted as though you believed that we were going to win."

"If you act as if you're going to win, then you're going to go a long way toward winning," Hebert concluded. And how does a coach convey that confidence? "I think the communication you send out as a coach, the body language, the gestures, voice tone...packs in a great deal about what you expect of them."

Research bears him out. Dr. Robert Rosenthal is famous for his "Pygmalion" experiment in 1964. Teachers were told that a certain group of children had been identified as particularly bright in psychological tests, while another group had been shown to have less remarkable ability. In fact, both groups had scored similarly on tests.

But sure enough, at the end of the year the "exceptional" children had shown greater achievement. Dr. Rosenthal theorized that, through body language and verbal cues, the teachers had favored the students they thought were the brightest. Since then, the same effect has been demonstrated in factories and offices and on athletic teams.

The message for coaches is clear: If you expect great things from your players, they're more likely to deliver great performance.

LOGISTICS

Hebert has made some personal observations about the effects of non-verbal communication. He and an assistant decided they would go to every championship event they could think of "to make notes on what we saw in every level, every aspect, every detail from how the team warmed up to how they walked into the gym. Was it together? Was it separately? When did the coaches come out? What did they do? How did they address their players in time-outs?" This meticulous observation paid off in winning teams.

Body Language

One of the things Hebert noticed was the way a certain coach conveyed his attitude through non-verbal signals. He was a very gifted coach who established an athletic department that remained at a high level long after he was gone. If you watched this coach on the side lines, you could tell how things were going. If things were going well, he was on the edge of his chair. When he was disgusted, he would slide down in his chair, legs crossed, head tilted to one side.

Hebert said the link between this coach's body language and the way his team played became so noticeable that it was hard to tell which was the cause and which was the effect.

This coach took his team to the Final Four seven times, but never won the national championship. His successor, using the same players, won it during his first year as coach. The first coach was taking the edge off his team with negative body language.

To give you some idea of the importance of non-verbal communication, consider that 80 percent of our waking hours is spent in face-to-face communication. But only 7% of our communication involves wording. The tone of voice, the pace of speech and the inflection of voice account for 38% of the meaning. Body language accounts for 55%.

Foul Expressions

My daughter has found non-verbal communication to be a drawback: When she played on her high-school basketball team, she used to get a lot of fouls. There were a couple of reasons. First, she played in the middle and she had very sharp elbows. Second, like her mother, she is a high I, and you can read everything she's thinking on her face. We used to say to her, "Dona, you've got to show a little less emotion; the ref knows when you're mad, and the minute anything happens over there you're going to get called."

Let's look at some of the factors that influence the way you're understood.

Instant Impressions

Your posture gives the other person an instant impression of you. The best posture, whether you're talking to a player or to a team, is to stand forward with your weight balanced on the balls of your feet. This will give you more energy and flexibility of movement and will make you look eager and enthusiastic. Don't rock back on your heels. That gives the impression that you're retreating.

You can convey a lot of meaning with your posture, but that's not all there is to it. You can lean forward and appear threatening. Or you can lean forward and appear interested in your listener. The difference? Facial expression is part of it. But there's also meaning in the hands. Closed fists are threatening. Open hands are accepting.

Jangling Nerves

Certain non-verbal mannerisms can be irritating to your listeners. Women should not play with their earrings when they're talking to someone. Come to think of it, men shouldn't either.

Women should also avoid playing with their hair. That's suggestive. They shouldn't tilt their heads. That's being coy as well as suggestive. And they shouldn't stand with their hands on their hips. They should stand quietly, using their hands to gesture.

Men shouldn't stand with hands in pockets, and they definitely shouldn't jingle their keys. Clipping fingernails while talking is also a no-no.

Making Eye Contact

Eye contact is important. Look directly at the person with whom you are communicating, whether you are talking or listening. Some people will look back at you. However, many people won't look you directly in the eye.

When I conduct a workshop, I find that many people look away when I look at them. But every once in a while they check back to see where my eye contact is. I don't give up immediately. I'll keep trying to establish eye contact, maybe for a couple of hours. If I haven't gotten it by then, I give up. I can't waste any more time and energy trying to engage them. I'll still check back every now and then, but I no longer try to include them in the way I do everybody else.

Breaking the Stare

At the opposite extreme is the starer. Nobody likes to be stared at while talking. You don't have to look away to break that off. Just blink. Blink every 15 to 20 seconds, and that establishes a break. If your listener has a stare fixed on you, your blink usually will give the signal for the starer to blink too.

It's usually best for the speaker and the listener to be at the same level. But occasionally, if you want to take control of a situation — establish dominance — it helps to stand while the listener is sitting. S and C coaches might want to remember that when dealing with D or I staffers and players.

IMPROVEMENTS

The National Institute of Business Management has compiled a number of tips on non-verbal communication.

If you're talking one-on-one and you're aiming for a longer, more relaxed chat, suggest that both persons sit. The chairs should be side by side or facing each other at an angle. A face-to-face arrangement suggests confrontation.

When talking to your team, the seating arrangement can be important. If you're aiming for an interchange of thought, with all members encouraged to join in, arrange the seats in a circle. A horseshoe or T shape focuses attention on those at the head of the configuration. Placing yourself at the center of the group invites everyone to participate.

If you're planning to do all the talking, and you want the team to sit and listen, arrange the chairs side by side as in a theater. If you use a podium or a raised speaker's platform, you're raising your status, but you're also making yourself less approachable. If you use a podium to establish yourself as the expert, you may later want to break the formality and ask for questions. A comfortable way to do this is to walk in front of the podium and invite the team to join the discussion.

Maintaining Good Voice Tone

Good voice tone is critical. People are unconsciously sensitive to sound, and they will be uncomfortable if the pitch is off. Learn to control your projection by taking adequate breaths and controlling the muscles of your diaphragm. Pace your words so you are not talking too quickly or too slowly. Too quickly frustrates; too slowly bores.

If your voice begins to rise, send your thoughts down through your body to your feet. Your breath will follow your awareness, and you will resume breathing through your diaphragm. This will deepen the tonal quality of your voice.

Moving Well

Use gestures and body movements to add emphasis to the points you want people to remember. Gesture during your statement. Such gestures look natural. Gestures that come before or after the point look contrived.

Don't raise your hands above your shoulders. It breaks eye contact, and it detracts from what you are saying. Don't point, shake your fingers, clench your fists or cross your arms. These gestures make you look angry and closed.

Controlling Without Words

We can convey many subtle and not-so-subtle messages without saying a word. Say you're talking to your pitching coach and the catcher approaches. Is it all right for this new person to join the conversation?

If you're facing the pitching coach in such a way that your bodies form two sides of an incomplete triangle, the message is, "Come on over and complete the triangle." If the catcher's behavior style is D, that should be all the invitation needed. If your foot points outward instead of directly at the pitching coach, your D or I person will then also feel free to join you. If you're dealing with an S, an outward glance or smile may do it. If that doesn't work, give an overt signal. Even the reclusive C will pick up on that.

Would you rather keep this a tête-à-tête between you and your assistant?

Stand close to and face your aide directly, forming a box. Point your feet directly at the assistant, and keep your eye contact with that person only. That should do for most behavior types. However, you may have to wave off a high D.

Ending the Talk

You can signal that a conversation is over in a number of ways. Look away from the person you've been talking to. Stand up; that's usually tantamount to announcing that "this discussion is terminated." Shift away from the face-to-face position, step backward or adjust your tie or jewelry. Glance at your watch.

Some people have found it effective to touch the other person while preparing to part. It's a cordial style of dismissal. Brushing imaginary lint off your suit is another way of saying, "I'm getting ready to leave." Rubbing your hands together as if getting rid of dust also signals that it's time to go.

Setting the Stage

You can even give non-verbal clues as to where a person should sit in a meeting. When you look at a certain seat or a certain section of the room, your glance provides direction. Giving the person a slight directional touch on the back offers a cue. When you're already seated and you'd like the backfield coach to sit next to you, look at him. He'll catch your eye and your drift.

Beware of the clumsy gestures that telegraph unfriendliness or give people the idea that they are being manipulated. Frowning, blatantly ignoring someone or placing your briefcase on the seat next to you constitutes bad manners and gives unfavorable impressions.

Running the Show

When you're meeting with the team, just by using your eyes you can exert a great deal of control over who does the speaking. If you want to give your high-I center a chance to speak, look at her. If she drones on and on and you want to stop her, look away from her. If you want to encourage your S catcher to keep pounding his point home, nod slightly, lean forward a little and smile. If you want your C line coach to explain a point, just raise an eyebrow, knit your brow or cock your head to the side. If you want your D offensive coach to stop belaboring a point, look away momentarily, shift your position or move your foot up and down rapidly.

Taking a Stand

Occasionally, S or C coaches may want to step out of their core styles and display dominance. You'll appear more aggressive if you stand straight, thrust out your chest and use your arms to stake out as much space as possible for yourself.

If you're in the audience and you want to show deference toward the person who's conducting the meeting, you can get the floor by raising your hand, clearing your throat or leaning forward expectantly.

If you're just trying to be friendly, try holding a palm outward. Gently touching the other person is another option.

Tensed muscles, clenched fists and pursed lips convey negative, threatening messages to your listeners. If you're under stress and you want to give your team an upbeat talk, try walking around a little, stretching, breathing deeply. Face the players in a loose, relaxed manner and you'll find a more receptive audience.

When addressing the team, pay attention to your personal appearance. Dress well. It will give you confidence, and that confidence will come through in your body language.

READING OTHERS' CUES

The non-verbal behavior of others can give you important clues as to what's going on among your players and staff.

Potential Face-Offs

You can spot a confrontation in the making by being on the alert for dominance-style behavior. If two persons look each other in the eye, without smiling, for longer than usual, you can infer that a test of wills is in the making. If they spend a lot of time discussing a minor point, watch out for clashing egos. If they face one another with hands on hips or thumbs in belts, sparks may be ready to fly.

If you want to head off the confrontation, find a way to divert the individuals to other pursuits. Laps and push-ups or a round of solitary practice may be effective. But at times you may decide that it's best to let things come to a head. Your I quarterback and D center may need to get the air cleared between them. Or your S catcher may need some encouragement to stand up to your D pitcher.

Wasted Rah-Rahs

If you notice people crossing and recrossing legs, shifting in their chairs or otherwise moving about, assume that your pep talk is going nowhere. You may be wasting your rah-rahs on a bunch of perfectionist Ss and Cs who just want you to tell them how you want the job done.

Stare Wars

If you get into a heated discussion with a D athlete or staffer and it ends with the two of you trying to stare each other down, who breaks eye contact first?

If you "outstare" your "adversary," don't take that as an indication of victory. Dr. Allan Mazur, professor of sociology at Syracuse University, says people of higher status usually break contact first; they take the lead in everything. Try to stay away from "stare wars."

Hints

Here are some other non-verbal signs and situations to look for:

• When there are vacant, bored looks, folded arms, downward looks, frowns or eyes searching the room for someone else to talk to, that indicates boredom and wandering attention. Direct questions can bring the wandering mind back to attention.

• When your tight end says, "Uh-huh, I get it," but rubs one eye, it's time for doubts. Rubbing one eye often indicates an inward refusal to accept something.

• When your ace pitcher tells you, with a determined look, of being ready to pitch the championship game, watch the feet. If they're beating up and down, they're contradicting the face, and they're probably right.

• When the assistant principal assures you that the new uniforms will be ready in time for the Homecoming Game, look at the forefinger and thumb of the left hand. If they're rubbing together, there's something being held back. Maybe the suits are the wrong color.

• When you're trying to persuade your running back to switch to linebacker, pay attention to the player's non-verbal signals. If the player stares at the ceiling and blinks rapidly, the possibility is being considered. Provide time for thinking. If you hear a deep breath and sighs, the mind is made up. Ask for an opinion, and if it corresponds with yours, get the player to commit before that changes.

A Word About Liars

Liars may unmask themselves in a number of ways. One is through a crooked smile; most genuine smiles are symmetrical. Another is through a smile, frown or look of disbelief that lasts too long. Most genuine expressions last only four or five seconds.

Failure to look you in the eye may be a sign of lying. Forced eye contact may mean the person is trying to fake it. Frequent rubbing of the nose is another possible tip-off. Fleeting expressions that are quickly covered by phony expressions also are indications that what has been spoken may not be the gospel. But be cautious: Some people have naturally crooked smiles, noses do occasionally itch and need scratching, some people are naturally averse to eye contact and fleeting expressions may be signs of wandering minds.

A Final Note

There is one main thing to be aware of: It's okay to observe, but don't do it obviously. Take frequent snapshots of your audience. Avoid prying looks.

Body language is a rich and fascinating mode of expression. Those who master its subtleties are on to an effective way of communicating the winning spirit.

8

Communicating with Style

Billy Martin (1987) said it best:

> You have to know when to tell players they screwed up without hurting them. How do you know? I can't answer that. It's one of those things that have to come instinctively. (p. 109)

When coaches and managers take the time to learn the behavior styles of their players, they take much of the guesswork out of communicating with them. They know to use different approaches in teaching the impatient D and the methodical S. They know that the fun-loving I requires a different kind of motivation from the perfectionist C.

But regardless of whom we are motivating, we need to communicate. And although a coach can communicate a lot through body language, and although wordless signals have become an effective medium on the baseball field, the spoken language remains the principal means of communicating among humans. Later in this chapter we will review some essentials for communicating with individual behavior styles, but at the outset, let's look at oral communication in general.

We all know what we mean when we say something. But what we mean isn't always what our listeners hear. They are hearing us through a membrane that embodies their social background, attitudes, education, beliefs, values and experiences. That membrane can warp the message in subtle and unsubtle ways.

By the same token, when your listener responds to you, the message is shaped on the sending end by his or her background, beliefs, values and experiences and is filtered on the receiving end through the membrane of your own internal environment.

That's why it's important, in one-way communication especially, to choose your words carefully with your audience in mind. In two-way communication, it is important not only to consider what you're saying, but also to listen carefully to the response. Your listener's response will tell you whether your message has been accurately received. But you must listen carefully, taking into consideration the factors that shape the meaning of the words you hear.

GOOD LISTENING

All of this means that to be a good communicator, you have to be a good listener.

Listening generates ideas. The most effective method a coach can use to gain fresh ideas is to listen attentively during formal and informal conversations throughout the day. Of course, if you are to benefit from these conversations, you must encourage your staff and players to communicate with you. They must feel free to ask questions, volunteer ideas and explain their problems to you.

If you're like most people, you talk "at" instead of "with" your conversational partners. The common attitude is that listening consists of trying to figure out as fast as possible the central point of the speaker's message. The trouble is, you often grasp what you think is the central idea, then tune out the rest of what is said. You're too busy preparing your response to hear what the speaker is saying. So instead of replying to what the speaker meant, you reply to what you heard — or thought you heard.

Both the speaker and the listener must assume some basic responsibilities if effective communication is to take place.

Communicating with Style

The Listener's Responsibilities

As a responsible listener, you should:

• Show by your actions that you are interested in what the speaker has to say and that you want to listen.

• Take the time to listen, and be sure you are ready.

• Try to learn something. Be positive rather than negative. Take a "this is an opportunity" approach when you listen.

• Get the whole message. Ask the speaker to repeat or clarify; ask who, what, when, where, why and how.

• Avoid interrupting the speaker. Let the speaker finish completely. Make mental or written notes of what you want to say without tuning out the sender. Evaluate your understanding of the message.

• Concentrate on listening. Position yourself to ward off distractions. Have the desire to listen. Look at the sender. Don't fidget, shuffle papers, clean your fingernails, open your mail or indulge in other discourtesies.

The Speaker's Responsibilities

Speakers, of course, have obligations to:

• Show the listener, by your actions, that you want attention. Be encouraging. Show that it is important to listen and prepare the receiver to listen.

• Be sure the listener is taking the time and is ready to listen. The timing of your message is essential.

• Try not to waste the listener's time.

• Give the listener the whole message (all the listener should know). Carefully plan your message around who, what, when, where, why and how.

• Repeat and clarify the main idea, problem, issue, question and facts. Avoid clutter.

• Position yourself and the listener to avoid distractions.

• Avoid personal habits or mannerisms that could distract while you are sending the message.

• Look at the listener.

• Evaluate the listener's interpretation of the message by requiring feedback. Ask specific questions about the message, or have the listener repeat and explain your message.

Although it is important for any speaker to be as non-ambiguous as possible, it is the listener who has the major, if not final, control over effective and meaningful communication. The listener is the feedback link in the communication process.

GUIDELINES FOR SPEAKERS

The first guideline for the speaker is to stick to the subject. Be specific, not vague. When you're talking to your shortstop about lack of hustle on the field, don't confuse the issue by commenting on this athlete's batting stance, behavior on the bench, low grades or food fighting in the cafeteria. Stick to the fielding.

If the shortstop wants to turn to another subject — the number of bases stolen, perhaps — just say, "Wait a minute; we need to finish talking about your fielding before we take up your base running."

Don't let discussions break down into nagging, arguing or repetitious criticism. It's okay to disagree. A little argument is inevitable. But we all know when we've reached the point that no agreement is likely. Sometimes we try to wear others down until they wearily throw in the towel. That is not good communication. It may be getting your way, but it's not communication. The person who is badgered into agreement will store the episode away and sooner or later come back at you. We call that collecting stamps. You collect a stamp and put it in your pocket, and you save it until you want to use it.

Be Fair

When you do argue, be fair about it. Don't try to score points by dredging up things that have nothing to do with what you're arguing about. If you're arguing with your spouse about the fact that you don't have enough money, it isn't fair to add, "and besides that, you don't take out the garbage," or, "and furthermore, I can't stand your broccoli casserole." If you're arguing with your forward over rebounding, don't add, "and besides that, I don't like the way you make your jump shot."

When you recognize that you're not going to carry your point in an argument and you're not willing to surrender the field completely, say, "Okay. How can we negotiate a solution?"

Remember what a conversation is: two-way communication. That means you have to share the floor. There's really no such thing as a one-way conversation. When one person monopolizes the talk, it becomes a lecture, a tirade or a monologue. No one likes a person who hogs the show.

Skillful communicators respect their audience's feelings and dignity. They may not agree with all ideas, but they still value listeners as persons. This is particularly necessary when you're dealing with sensitive S and I persons. Since they are motivated by the desire to be liked, you destroy their morale when you attack their dignity and self-respect.

Realize They May Not Know

Don't assume that everyone knows what you're talking about. Things that seem second-nature to you may be novel concepts to your listener. Information that has long been logged and cataloged in your mind may be absent from your hearer's mind.

I once attended a meeting of a fund-raising committee as a newcomer. The chairman kept speaking in half sentences. He would start a sentence and end it with "you know...." As a new member, I assumed that everyone else knew what he was talking about, so I kept quiet for a while to avoid showing my ignorance. But after about 20 minutes of "you knows" I finally spoke up: "I'm sorry, Jim, but I don't know what you're talking about. I've just joined the organization and I'm new on the committee." Know what? Nobody else on that committee knew what Jim was talking about either. He assumed everybody knew, but nobody did.

How can you tell whether your listeners understand you? You ask them. You watch them. Some people are good at faking attention. Others will tell you they understand when they really don't. So after you've explained things, say to your listener, "Okay. Tell me what you understand you're supposed to do."

Don't Dictate

Nobody likes a dictator. So when you're talking to your players or staff, it's usually best to avoid the "Do as I say" approach. Give your point of view as information, not as law. If others offer different ideas, hear them out.

Of course, there comes a time when the coach has to decide which way things will be done; there are times when the coach's word must be law. That message can be conveyed without savaging the self-respect of subordinates. You can, for instance, acknowledge that your way isn't the only way and that other good suggestions have been advanced. But state that after considering all alternatives, you've reached a conclusion you believe to be best overall. And indicate that's the conclusion that will govern. The message you thereby convey is not "My word is law," but rather "The buck stops here."

Clarify Meanings

When you do lay down the law, make sure that everyone understands what the law is. Once when I told my daughter to clean her room before going out on Saturday night, I discovered that the word "clean" means a different thing to teen-agers than it does to adults: I had to go behind her and clean it myself to demonstrate to her the meaning of the word as I understood it.

It's amazing how slippery meanings can be. The 500 most-used words in the English language can have 14,000 different meanings. For instance, if you invite friends over for dinner, make sure you know what part of the country they're from. In some localities, dinner is the noon meal, and supper is what you eat in the evening. Where I live, dinner is the evening meal. In some areas, a mess of beans is what you have when you spill a plate of limas on the dining-room carpet. In other places, it's the quantity of beans needed to make a meal.

Accentuate the Positive

Avoid focusing on negative aspects. We don't have to ignore them, but we should focus on the solution rather than the problem. Instead of saying, "Jan, your free-throw average is the pits," say, "Jan, let's see if we can find a way to add a few points to your free-throw average." Working on the solution is what keeps things moving and growing.

When a person has a problem, always attack the problem and not the person. When you start your conversation with "You always," "You should" or "You never," you're attacking the person.

And the person can usually come up with an answer:

"Bill, you always hit straight into the left fielder's glove when you try to pull the ball against Lefty Parker's curve."

"No I don't. I hit a triple to right the last time I went up against him."

"Doris, you always lose possession when you try to pass the ball behind you."

"Not true. I can name at least a dozen times when I did it and set up a score."

How about this:

"Bill, let's see if we can't take some of the sting out of Lefty's curve ball. Instead of trying to pull it to left, why don't you try just meeting the ball and laying it into left center."

Or, try this: "Doris, when you're trying to set up a play, why not go with your strength: Pass the ball in front of you."

Avoid Anger

Anger is probably the emotion that blocks more communication than anything else. Some people automatically get their danders up when others disagree. Such people will find it hard to communicate.

Often the anger can be defused just by learning why a person holds a different opinion. The person's background, experience and behavior style may be at the root of the opinion. Coaches dealing with young athletes should be particularly wary of venting anger until they are aware of home conditions, family relationships and other problems. The girl who walks out of the gym a bit early every day may not be evidencing a lack of dedication. She may be going home to an abusive parent who gets violent if she comes in after sundown.

When others show anger, it's best if you can keep your cool and calm them down. Show the angry person that you're sympathetic: "I know that this is upsetting you, Diane." Sometimes this simple acknowledgment can relieve hurts and put people in a mood to work things out. You're telling them that their feelings are important to you and you're willing to pay attention to what they say. It doesn't mean you agree with them—just that you're willing to work toward a mutually agreeable solution.

Abandon Preconceived Notions

We should always abandon preconceived notions when dealing with individuals. Not all Italians eat pasta three times a day and hobnob with the Mafia. Not all Irish are hot-tempered. Not all blacks love rap music. Not all Hispanic men are macho. A speech impediment or a hearing impairment has absolutely no bearing on a person's mental or athletic ability.

We should keep in mind the other person's perspective, though. When you read in your newspaper that a public figure lives in a posh apartment, what does it mean? Probably that the apartment is more expensive than the one the reporter lives in.

What's an expensive car? If you drive a 10-year-old VW, it may be a brand-new Honda. If you drive a new Honda, it may be a Cadillac. If you drive a Cadillac, it may be a Rolls Royce. It's all in your perspective.

When your teen-ager describes someone as an "older person," you should not imagine a tottering old man or a little old lady in a walker. To teen-agers, an "older person" is someone in their parents' generation. In the Army, a grizzled veteran is someone at least in the late 40s. In major-league baseball, you become a grizzled veteran somewhere in your late 20s. On Main Street, a 200-pound person is considered hefty. On the front four of an NFL team, that's a lightweight. At a cocktail party, 6-foot-4 is considered tall. On an NBA team, even a 6-foot-6 player will be called "shorty."

Police have to be careful when witnesses give them descriptions of suspects. If they describe a white male of average height, how tall is he? The average height for a male in the United States (not in the NBA) is 5-foot-8. But my husband is 6-foot-2. To me, a man of average height stands, oh, about 6-foot-2.

So when you're listening, listen from the perspective of the speaker. When someone says, "I'm a good hitter," it's helpful to know whether the speaker is a pitcher or an outfielder. The difference may be 100 points or more in batting average.

Learn to Ask

One of the most useful skills in communicating is the asking of questions. You set the tone for a conversation with the questions you ask. When people respond to a question, they tend to follow the questioner's lead. If you ask direct questions, you set the tone for a no-nonsense talk. Direct questions elicit direct answers.

Avoid accusatory tones unless you really want to put someone on the defensive: "You normally put your volleyball serves right where you want them, Sylvia, but lately I've noticed your accuracy is a little off. Are you having trouble with your concentration?"

If you're clear with your questions and include specific examples, you encourage your respondent to be specific as well.

If it's really a knotty problem, and you want to minimize your respondent's discomfort, start with the easier questions. Simpler questions put people at ease and enable them to be more open when the harder questions come. When you walk into an office and are confronted with a volley of tough, accusatory questions, your composure may fly out the window.

But if the questioner leads up to the major questions, you have time to think and prepare a rational response.

The skillful communicator uses silence as well as words. Train yourself to stop and count slowly to five every once in a while. Although you may feel uncomfortable sitting in silence, it gives the other person more thinking time. Your respondent may fill the silent space with information that might not have been volunteered otherwise.

When to Say It

In communicating with athletes, timing is important, especially when what you have to say involves criticism or correction.

When D persons do something that needs correcting, the time to speak is immediately. Decisiveness is what counts with them. With I persons, it's best to wait until you can meet with them in private. With S persons, take the time to develop logical introductions, showing how your counsel fits into their concepts. With C people, take a moment to assure them that you value them as persons before you deal with their athletic performance.

TALKING TO Ds

D persons are motivated by a fear of losing. This fear may stem from a feeling of inadequacy. D persons are accustomed to being commended only when they have succeeded. Hence, their self-esteem is closely tied in with success. They fear that if they lose they will be rejected. So when you communicate with D players, you need to stress their value apart from their performance on the field.

"I know it hurts to go 0 for 4 in a big game, Darryl, but your hustle always sets an example for the whole team. With you out there, I know the others are going to be playing a couple of notches above average."

Even when D athletes really flub, it's often best to let them fail without criticism. They need to know you approve of them even when they're not creaming the opposition.

When you're teaching D athletes, remember this: They're impatient. They don't want to be bothered by irrelevant details. Give them the basic steps and let them start practicing. They don't like to waste words or time.

When you want to compliment Ds, mention their achievements and leadership potential. Don't bother to tell them what nice people they are. They don't want to hear that; they want to hear how successful they are.

When you're discussing problems with them, draw them into the solutions. Ds have an urge to be top banana. They'll act much more vigorously when they have part ownership of the idea. Be ready to listen to their suggestions and to incorporate them into the solutions where practicable.

If you're a D person, cultivate the art of active listening. Ds tend to shut out small talk. Impatient with details, they frequently make decisions without getting the whole story. But to help your athletes, you need to hear what's on their minds. Only then can you give them wise direction. Steer away from the easy answers and quick decisions. Look for long-term solutions.

The D person's attitude is marked by supreme self-confidence. D people don't need ego massages. They therefore assume that other people don't either.

But other people do. The people-oriented Is and Ss particularly need constant assurance that they are admired or liked. If you want to motivate them, compliment them. D people don't like to waste time repeating themselves. But others may need constant assurance. So you told your I runner yesterday what a splendid sprinter she was? That was yesterday. She needs to hear it today. And she'll need to hear it tomorrow. Indulge her. It will pay off in more victories.

PRAISING THE I

For the I person, the key to motivation is admiration. I athletes love the limelight, love to be admired. Compliment them often. With the D athlete, you praise the accomplishments. With the I, it's all right to praise the person.

Don't deride their love for acclaim as empty egotism. Let them enjoy their place in the sun. Every team can benefit from the presence of athletes who do their best when the spotlight is on them.

The I person doesn't have the D person's aversion to

small talk. Small talk, indeed, can put the I into a competitive mood. As Mary Lou Retton remarked, "I'd come in some days when the last thing I wanted to do was work out, and Bela would see that and start making jokes, massaging my shoulders and getting me pumped up" (Retton and Karolyi, 1986, p. 79).

I persons, more than the other behavior types, will respond to pep talks. They're natural cheerleaders themselves. They thrive in optimistic environments.

Like D persons, though, they don't want to be bothered with details. When teaching the I athlete, avoid complexities. Focus on the big picture.

Remember that the morale destroyer for Is is public embarrassment. The wise coach will be particularly careful to avoid embarrassing them in front of friends. If you need to confront them about their mistakes, do it in private and do it in a non-threatening way.

The I person's urge to entertain may be disruptive at practices. If this becomes a problem, a serious talk may be in order. Here, the objective should be to convince the I that he or she doesn't have to win love through entertaining behavior. It's possible to be liked for who you are as well as for what you do. The I's penchant for trying new techniques before mastering them may be remedied wordlessly by allowing the athlete to try them and fail repeatedly before others.

The I coach needs to be aware of the natural tendency in those of this behavior style to stay on the good side of others. This can be a drawback when it comes to making tough personnel decisions. When a pitcher loses control, a quarterback loses edge or a forward's shots go flat, it's no time for bonhomie. It's time to do what's best for the team. The I needs to borrow some objectivity from the C behavior style.

AFFIRMING THE S

The S loves approval and hates conflict. Anything other than a peaceful relationship tells S people they've failed. They are not motivated by the need to win, but by the need to be liked. So the successful coach will repeatedly assure S people that they are highly regarded, and he or she will try to establish friendly relations with them.

S people make good listeners. They pay attention to what you're saying, and they try to do things the way they're told. Use a logical approach with them, showing how your message fits in with their view of things.

S people will try to master skills one step at a time. They will want to perfect one step before going on to the next. Unlike the D, who likes to get it right the first time, the S needs frequent repetition and hands-on demonstration. Pictures and drawings also are helpful teaching tools. Each time Ss try and succeed, assure them that they're doing fine. They want to be certain they won't look foolish when they attempt something new.

The S coach needs to learn assertiveness. Nobody is going to be liked at all times by all people. At times, it's necessary to risk disapproval to get the job done. At team practice, disrespectful athletes need to be challenged and corrected. That may cause tension, but avoiding the conflict won't solve the problem.

The S coach also needs to learn to deal with anger. S people have a tendency to withdraw in angry silence from an argument or a conflict situation. It's best not to internalize your anger or to use silence as a weapon.

INFORMING THE C

Like the extroverted Ds, C athletes don't respond well to the "rah-rah" approach to motivation. If you want to get them charged up, compliment their performance, and let them know that you respect them as persons—then tell them how to improve their games. And be prepared for questions.

When C athletes ask questions, they're not being defensive and are not engaging in idle talk. They're asking for clarification. Answer them directly, in a non-threatening voice, with neutral body language. Give them as much detail and as many reassurances as possible.

C persons want to know where they fit into the big picture. They need clearly defined areas of responsibility. Given that, they will conscientiously and methodically fulfill their responsibilities.

The big downer for them is criticism of their work. As perfectionists, they identify closely with the quality of their performance. When you're criticizing their performance, you're criticizing them. Therefore, it's doubly necessary to approach them from the positive side. Don't fault them for batting .240. Talk to them about ways to get their average up to .300.

The C coach needs to cultivate some of the D's decisiveness. It isn't always necessary to have all the information in hand before deciding to act. As Joe Paterno learned in the Sugar Bowl, it sometimes pays to trust the intuition.

C persons also need to learn to share their expertise and be tolerant of others' failings. C coaches, like their D counterparts, need to cultivate the art of the compliment.

THE WINNING COMBINATION

We dealt in an earlier chapter with the dilemma of the coach whose pep talk affected different players in different ways.

When deciding how to motivate your team in the locker room or at time-outs, it's helpful to know the behavior styles of the players. If you're dealing with a preponderance of Cs, go heavy on the practical pointers, mixing in a little praise for what they're doing right. If you're dealing with a lot of Ss, appeal to them on the basis of team spirit, and tell them exactly how you want them to play the game. If you're dealing with Is, pour on the rah-rah, you-can-do-it steam. With Ds, make it a challenge: That crowd doesn't think you can do it. That other team thinks you're soft. Go show 'em!

At Illinois, Mike Hebert didn't give up when he found that his pep talk turned off his C players and high S perfectionists. Instead, he looked around at his coaching staff. He decided that he and his assistants would share the time-out duties.

When the team came off the floor for a time-out huddle, his C assistant would talk to the center, who was also a C person. The assistant would give the player practical pointers on improving her game. A graduate assistant, also a C, would talk to the other perfectionists. Hebert, who is an I, would take the rest. Toward the end of the time-out, Mike would address the whole team with a few words of encouragement. Then the women would return to the floor.

With a good knowledge of your players, you should be able to tailor your team talks to the behavior styles you're trying to influence. Learn the proper mix: challenge for the Ds, rah-rah for the Is, team spirit for the Ss, and practical advice for the Cs.

The informed coach can put together a winning motivational combination.

9

Winning Over Stress

Most coaches and athletes view their lives as inherently stressful. In no other line of endeavor is success tied so directly to winning at competition.

Stress can be positive as well as negative. The thrill of the challenge when your team enters championship competition is a form of positive stress. It motivates you to give that extraordinary effort that distinguishes champions from also-rans.

Negative stress, though, can poison a team's victory prospects. Coaches know that a team that enters a contest anxious and tense goes in at a disadvantage. If the other team is relaxed and loose, its state of mind may be enough to offset advantages of talent, size and experience.

Negative stress is an enemy, whether in a family, vocational or athletic situation. It saps energy, destroys motivation and generates mistakes. It also causes illness.

Stress is an enemy of concentration, which is essential to athletic success. It eats away at performance in competition. It impedes learning in the clubhouse and on the practice field.

A COMMON OCCURRENCE

Mike Hebert says stress is pervasive among college athletes.

"Every time I tell the team, 'Let's be nutritionally sound,' it's just bouncing off a wall because their sensors are not tuned in," said the University of Illinois volleyball coach. "They carry around the symptoms of stress. We know that thoughts race uncontrolled through our minds. We're unable to focus for longer than literally three to five minutes. That's the most that most people can focus on one task. We can't read as well because we can't synthesize."

Why do we encounter so much stress? For one thing, the human body was designed for simpler challenges. When the mind perceives a challenge, it puts the body on alert. The body goes taut, waiting to confront the challenge. That's stress.

In the primitive stage of the human experience, the challenge may have been the approach of a lion or bear. The body had to be prepared to fight or to flee. So the cave dweller's glands pumped adrenaline into the blood, more sugar became available for energy, the number of red blood cells increased to accept a greater charge of oxygen, the breathing quickened to provide the extra oxygen and the heart pumped faster to speed this emergency fuel to the muscles. To use a modern analogy, the cave dweller's engine raced and the system went into passing gear.

These are emergency responses. Once the bear moved on, or the cave dweller had fled to a safe retreat, the brain's alarm system shut down and things returned to normal.

If the system remains permanently keyed up for emergencies, things begin to break down. If you run your automobile constantly in passing gear at full throttle, it will reach the junk heap long before you've made your last payment.

Modern "Bears"

Modern people no longer worry about encountering a bear, unless they happen to be confronting the Chicago team in the NFL. Our stress causer is more likely to be the postal carrier with the monthly bills, the school superintendent with a budgetary cutback, the assistant coach with a chip on the shoulder or a star fullback with a pulled leg muscle.

Cave dwellers' challenges came and went quickly, and if they survived, they could relax until the next bear came along. Modern challenges are not so fleeting. They loom in our consciousness for days and weeks and months. Our bodies react the same way they would react to the approach of a bear. But we're running flat out in passing gear for much longer periods. And the challenges are more numerous and more complex.

UNAVOIDABLE STRESS

You may not be able to do much about the stresses that assault you and your players. But you can do something about the way you respond to that stress. And you can take some simple, common-sense steps to minimize the effects of stress.

Staying Healthy

Here are some basic suggestions for handling on-the-job stress:

• Start your day with breakfast. Occasionally, arrange to meet a friend or co-worker for breakfast, and take the time to enjoy it.

• Drink water or fruit juice instead of coffee and carbonated beverages.

• Organize your work. When you sit down each morning, make a list of things you need to do, and arrange them in priority. Write things down; don't overburden your memory.

• Cut yourself some slack. Don't insist that everything you do be letter-perfect.

• Don't try to do too many things at once.

• Instead of taking work home with you, come in a little earlier or stay a little later occasionally.

• Reduce the noise level in your office. Rugs and draperies can help.

• If the telephone is a frequent interruption, have your calls held when you are extra busy.

- Plan for uninterrupted blocks of time to tackle big jobs or a collection of small ones.

- In a respectful way, let others know how you feel about petty annoyances.

- Develop support networks with co-workers. How much of your peak workloads can be shared? The inability to delegate responsibility can contribute to stress. People who insist on doing everything themselves often suffer from information overload, then burnout. Are you paying attention, Ss and Cs?

- When you take a break, leave your job behind. Get out and explore your city on foot at lunchtime. Have lunch with a co-worker or friend. Take 10- to 20-minute meditation breaks during lunch hour.

- Follow good nutrition, and get plenty of exercise, sleep and rest.

- Analyze the balance between work, rest and recreation. Make adjustments where needed.

Understanding Styles

Much of the stress we encounter comes from our interrelations with others, in our families and on the job. Our understanding of the different behavior styles can help us minimize on-the-job stress. If we understand our own behavior style and the styles of others, we can better understand different forms of behavior.
- If we know that Dean is a high D, we will accept his strong ego as a part of his personality and will understand that his boastful tendency is not an attempt to put us down.
- If we know that Imogene is a high I, we will understand her tendency to be disorganized and will not assign her tasks that require meticulous attention to detail.
- We will save those tasks for Charles, who is a high C and whose foot-dragging on urgent tasks drives us up the wall. We will give the urgent tasks to Imogene, who excels at doing

things well at the last minute, or to Dean, who will probably delegate them to Shirley.
* Shirley, the steady S, will get the job done and do it well. We'll learn not to fret over her occasional tendency to withdraw. Instead, we'll give her regular praise and affirmation and will encourage her to be assertive.

When we know where people are coming from, it's easier to deal with their human traits. It's the unknown that causes us stress.

CAUSES OF STRESS

Look around for stress-causing situations in your organization. Do you delegate responsibility without providing the authority or the resources to exercise that responsibility? That generates stress. Do you keep the rewards in line with the responsibility? That minimizes stress.

Conflicts

Conflicts among staffers are frequent sources of stress. If the conflicts involve Ds and Is, you'll probably learn about them quickly enough. Ss and Cs may keep their squawks to themselves, maintaining serene exteriors while the fires burn inside. Either way, productivity and team effort suffer.

The way to handle conflicts is to talk them out openly and honestly. Don't be afraid to broach the subject with extroverted Ds and Is. Make extra efforts to establish trusting relationships with introverted Ss and Cs. That will make it easier for you to spot smoldering conflicts and bring them safely into the open.

The Screaming Blunderbuss

Sometimes stress is the parent of irrational behavior. Coaches who scream invectives at their players, rip off their ties and fling their coats around are engaging in irrational behavior. What does it accomplish?

The answer is "nothing." Many coaches believe this kind of behavior gets their teams fired up. But many successful coaches manage to motivate without blowing their composure.

And even Bobby Knight has admitted, "Sometimes I regret it when the chair's half-way across the floor" (Mellen, 1989, p. 52). Most teams are made up of a variety of behavior styles. Coaching smart is learning what motivates each style and working that motivation into your approach to the team. Coaching dumb is ranting and raving without worrying about how it's affecting different individuals. A relaxed coaching staff will create a less stressful environment for the athletes.

Also, remember, many of your athletes may come from home and social environments that generate stress. The athlete must learn to deal with this stress also.

Signs of Stress

Stress announces itself in several overt ways. The athlete showing signs of fatigue, insomnia, indigestion, diarrhea or headaches may be suffering from stress. Frequent irritability is a telling sign. Night sweats, damp palms, cold extremities and rapid heartbeat are other indicators. If athletes seem shaky, weak or unsteady, or they show signs of shallow breathing and hyperventilation, stress is a likely suspect.

The person under stress may have irrational thought patterns or fears, may have trouble thinking clearly and may be unable to concentrate on a task.

Avoidable Stress

Certain types of stress are avoidable. Among them is negative self-chatter.

"What an idiot I am!" says Charlotte, the high C. "Why can't I dig that ball?"

The alert coach can help Charlotte in two ways:

(1) Convince her that she can be very good without being perfect and that, as far as the coach is concerned, being very good is more than satisfactory.

(2) Show her how to dig the ball.

Athletes often are plagued by anxiety-producing thoughts and fears:

"What if we lose this match?" frets Doris.

"Basketball isn't fun any more; am I doing the right thing?" wonders Ian.

"I am so tired and beat up, I'll never make it," laments Sharon.

"Maybe our team isn't that good," worries Cameron.

The Sun also Rises

Doris needs to understand that if her team loses the match, the sun will rise on schedule, her parents will still love her and the coach will still be her friend. Her worth does not depend upon her athletic performance.

Ian needs a little pumping up, a little praise for his rebounding skills, his defensive play and his ability as a playmaker.

Sharon needs a friendly ear and some fatherly or motherly assurance that she's an okay person who will be an asset to the team whether she leads in scoring or just steadies the other players with her presence.

Cameron needs to be complimented on his own proficiency and encouraged to let the coach bear the burden of others' imperfections.

Another source of stress on the team is the gripe session in which players dwell on the negative. Here's where the optimistic I coach or assistant can be a factor. Encourage the players to think positively. The team with the optimism is the team with the edge.

Bear-Shaped Rocks

Attitude is the critical factor in dealing with stress.

When the Neanderthal saw the bear, it wasn't the bear that caused the cave dweller's system to go on red alert. It was the person's perception of the bear. If the Neanderthals had seen a big rock and mistaken it for a bear, they would have experienced the same amount of stress. If they had seen a bear-shaped rock at every bend of the trail, their bodies would have remained in a constant state of stress, though they may actually have been in no danger at all.

In their daily lives, athletes are constantly encountering rocks that look like bears. The discerning coach learns to help players identify these phony dangers and put them out of mind.

The D player fears that losing will lead to rejection. That's a rock, not a bear.

The I player fears that one foolish play will lead to everlasting humiliation. That's a rock, not a bear.

The S player fears that standing up to D's aggressiveness or showing annoyance at C's pickiness will result in the loss of friends. That's a rock, not a bear.

The C player fears that decisive action might result in a mistake that will become a permanent blot on C's record. That's a rock, not a bear.

THE MIND

It's the unconscious mind that keeps us reacting to those bear-shaped rocks. It can't distinguish between perception and reality. Therefore, it orders our body to prepare for fight or flight, even when confronted with non-threatening realities. We need to reprogram the unconscious mind.

Programming the Unconscious

The unconscious mind is hard to define. The conscious mind is the one we deal with during our waking hours. It's the mind that lets us know that we exist; it's the one that tells us who we are and what we are experiencing.

But the unconscious mind is the computer that controls us. Like a computer, it is only as good as the data programmed into it. If it's properly programmed, it will properly serve us.

The unconscious mind becomes programmed by our thoughts and perceptions of reality over a lifetime. Bad programming can come from many sources:

• It can come from your childhood environment. If your parents wanted you to be a ballerina and you were born with two left feet, the message probably got logged into your unconscious mind fairly early: You can't dance, so you're undesirable.

• It comes from your own conscious rationalizations. The task looks insurmountable, so you tell yourself that, 1) you'll never be able to learn it, or 2) that you have so many other things to do that you'll never get around to trying it.

• It comes from a lifetime of negative thinking: "This town is the pits." "Who does she think she is, aiming for my position just because she's a half-inch taller?" "Here I go; probably going to screw up again...."

Since the unconscious mind is really in charge of your behavior, this negative programming gives a negative cast to your whole outlook. But if you have unwittingly implanted negative programming into your unconscious mind, take heart. You can also implant some positive programming. You can program your unconscious to make good things happen.

How do you do it?

Reaching the Alpha State

By concentrating on positive thoughts and by dreaming positive dreams. Your unconscious mind can be reached when your brain is in the alpha state, which is the relaxed state you enter when you daydream. About 80% of the time, your brain is in the beta state. That's the state of full alertness, when your brain waves are zooming along at between 14 and 60 cycles per second. The left brain dominates and you can do math, write essays, organize your schedules and do your income taxes.

The alpha state is reached when brain waves drop to between 7 and 14 cps. That's when you are at your most creative. The right brain takes over. You dream, relax or drift in a state of passive awareness. You are intuitive instead of rational in this state. You think in images and patterns instead of words. You can arrive at solutions to problems in a flash of insight instead of having to wriggle through a maze of logic.

In that state, you can reach your unconscious mind.

The unconscious mind will believe what it's told in the alpha state. So in this relaxed state, you want to keep your mind accentuating the positive. Keep telling yourself that you are what you want to be: a happy, calm, caring person; a healthy, positive, alert player; a person who can face adversity with confidence; a player who is supportive of teammates and who contributes to team goals.

Visualize yourself doing the things you want to do: pitching a shutout, hitting a perfect shot from the top of the key, getting the starting quarterback slot, sprinting to a new Olympic record.

Techniques for Relaxing

There are a number of techniques for achieving this level of serenity. Deep muscle relaxation — the deliberate tensing, then relaxing of key muscles in the body and face — can lower the tension in the body. Benson's Relaxation Technique, which involves quiet meditation and the repetition of a simple, neutral word or sound, can take tension from the mind (Benson, 1975, pp. 112-115).

In this relaxed state, your unconscious mind will be willing to believe the positive things you say about yourself, visualize about yourself and dream about yourself.

The coach can encourage such positive programming in several ways. One way is to make the team look like a winner. Sharp uniforms are great for instilling winning pride. Another way is to communicate optimism. Don't wait until the big game to pump up team morale. Encourage your players to practice as though they were going to win.

Know the Needs

Coaches who want to win will be aware of the behavior that produces negative stress among their athletes. They will know their players' behavior styles and will be aware of the ideal motivational environment for each style.

Here are some things to keep in mind about stress as it affects each behavior style:

• High Ds experience stress when they fail to meet their personal goals. They seek a physical release for their tensions, which means they often vent their stress through fits of anger. Understanding coaches will realize that Ds need to be in control of things. They will find ways of helping them release tension through physical activity. And they will look for ways to help them achieve their personal goals.

• High Is become more talkative under stress. They release nervous energy through physical exertion, but in a more emotional way than do the Ds. They need to maintain positive social relationships with their peers. Coaches can help them by encouraging them to spend time with others and talk out their problems. Sometimes an S teammate can provide a good listening ear. Usually, the optimistic I needs only a short time to recover from stress.

• High S athletes tend to hold stress inside. Conflict and change often are at the roots of their tension. "Sleeping it off" is one way S people relieve stress. Relief can come through other activities that give their minds some rest. Watching television, simple chores and walking can be helpful.

• High Cs prefer to tune out stress. They want to be alone. Since chaos is stressful to them, they need orderly environments with well-defined responsibilities to help them deal with tension. Discerning coaches will allow them their time alone, meanwhile reassuring them of continuing support. They may encourage the C to relieve stress through reading a book or pursuing a hobby.

Go With the Positive

Winning coaches will learn their own core behavior styles. They will try to emphasize the positive, productive traits of their core styles and downplay the less positive ones. They will help their staffs and their players do the same.

Successful coaches will recognize their roles as far more than developers of technique and strategy. They will see themselves as facilitators for pulling together all the physical, mental and emotional factors that turn good teams into winning teams.

And one of the things they need to teach their athletes is that life is not one big, long championship game. It is a series of events to be anticipated, savored and remembered, in victory and in defeat. There may be bears to fight out on the field or court, but they go home after the final whistle blows or the final out is made. Then it's time for the athlete to go home too — to the real life that exists off the playing field and that offers its own rich menu of challenges, rewards, achievements and thrills.

10

Creating a Winning Environment

An athletic team is more than just a collection of players directed by a staff of coaches. It is an organism made up of interacting parts. For the organism to prosper—to win—the parts must fit. They must meld into a smooth, functional blend.

The primary element in that blend is the coach. The coach is the person who establishes the environment for the team and its staff. Creating a winning environment requires more than the assembling of talent. That talent must be organized, mobilized and motivated.

Winning coaches will recognize the behavior styles of their staffs and players. They will learn to organize their staffs with attention to the roles for which each behavior style is best suited. They will learn how to motivate each individual.

But before you can do that, you must recognize your own behavior style. Know your strengths and weaknesses. Play to your strengths and shore up your weaknesses by leaning on the strengths of subordinates. Fortunately, coaching is one of those professions that does not favor one behavior style over another. You can be a successful coach regardless of your core style or your classical pattern.

To create a winning environment, you first create a setting in which people will want to win. Such an atmosphere will provide not only challenges, but also the tools for meeting those challenges, and it will provide pleasure and fulfillment when the challenges are met.

In this chapter, we will be looking for ways to achieve maximum loyalty and support from a coaching staff. Many of the suggestions spring from material compiled by The Research Institute of America and published in its special report, *Creating and Motivating a Superior, Loyal Staff*, copyrighted in June 1986. The Research Institute's material was aimed at management in general, but much of it is applicable to the coaching situation.

THE GOLDEN RULE

The best rule for establishing a winning environment is the Golden Rule: "Do unto others as you would have others do unto you."

That rule is practiced most effectively in the spirit instead of the letter. If you're a D person, the way you would want to be treated might be quite different from the way an S person would want to be treated. So we can try a little paraphrase of that time-tested rule: "Do unto others as they would have you do unto them."

That doesn't mean that you should put yourself at the absolute disposal of others. It means, rather, that you should understand others' behavior styles and let your dealings with them be guided by those styles in the spirit of the Golden Rule.

Be Flexible

In other words, the winning coach will be flexible in dealing with others. That doesn't mean you must adopt the behavior style of the person with whom you're dealing. Be yourself; don't be a phony. But adjust your approach to fit the style and temperament of the person with whom you are dealing.

Billy Martin (1987), that great model of flexibility, declared that a basic rule for any manager "is to manage according to his personnel. A good manager doesn't try to adapt his personnel to his style of managing; a good manager changes his style of managing to suit his personnel" (p. 16).

If you want a D person to perform some task for you, you may tell the individual directly, concisely and confidently what you want done.

If you ask an S person to perform the same task, you might want to spend a little time explaining the reason and logic behind what you're asking the individual to do.

Flexible coaches don't run an organization strictly for themselves. Every member has to feel that he or she is a part of the organization. As noted earlier, Rip Engle, Joe Paterno's predecessor at Penn State, advised his protégé, "Remember, it's their team, not yours." That means that the coach will be trying to meet the needs of others as well as those of herself or himself. If different preferences give rise to potential conflict, the coach will want to negotiate, with tact and with understanding.

Don't Toy with Authority

Horseplay is a natural by-product of the exuberance that goes with an athletic enterprise. The practical joke is a permanent fixture of locker rooms and gyms. But practical jokes often are funny only to the perpetrator. The wise coach will avoid using his authority to increase the emotional discomfort of others.

George Sisk had been having a good spring-training season as a relief pitcher with the New York Mets when manager George Bamberger called him in. Sisk had high hopes of making the roster.

"Sorry," said the manager, "but we're sending you back to the minors. Do you have anything you want to say?"

"No," said the rookie.

"That's good," said the manager, "because that's not how it is. You're staying."

The rookie's teammates, who had been listening outside the office door, broke into laughter over the momentary distress of the player. A coach should avoid toying with his or her authority in this way. Whereas the rookie might have found a good-natured way to "get even" with his peers, he might have found it risky to try to turn the tables on his boss (The Research Institute of America, 1986, p. 9).

Clarify Roles

An organization functions smoothly only when every component has a role and performs in accordance with that role. For this to take place, there has to be a common goal. That goal must be understood and accepted by everyone in the organization. If common understanding is not reached, you may have different people pulling in different directions, with disastrous results.

Staff

The winning coach will know the staff and how each member contributes toward the common goal. That means knowing what each staffer does. You don't learn that by constantly "checking up" on your subordinates, making sure that each staffer is in the proper place at precisely the proper time. You learn it by sharing experiences, ideas and feelings with them. Open communication is important. If you go day after day without sharing your thoughts with your subordinates, you create an atmosphere of suspicion. In such an atmosphere, teamwork breaks down.

The winning coach knows the staffers well enough to discuss with them their respective roles. Both coach and staffer should be clear on what those roles are. And if you know the role each staffer plays, it becomes easier to help a new staffer adapt.

Help Newcomers

As Martin (1987) observed, "You take a guy from another organization and he doesn't always fit in. He has different techniques, different habits, different coaching and instruction" (pp. 147-148).

The newcomer may also face an existing staff that is jealous of its turf. More established staffers have a sense of ownership about their jobs and may be fearful that the newcomer will try to take over some of their duties.

If the coach and staff have clear understandings of each staffer's role, the chances of conflict are diminished. What's more, the newcomer's adjustment period will be easier. She or he will be stepping into a clearly defined job. The individual's effort can be devoted to doing the job, not to learning what the job is.

One thing the coach can do for a newcomer is to make it clear that the new person's arrival marks the beginning of a new game. His or her predecessor may have been well-liked and respected. But from now on, things within the newcomer's bailiwick will be done the newcomer's way.

Provide a Piece of the Action

Winning coaches know how to make their staffs feel like winners. One way to do this is to cut the staff in on the action. Don't assume the role of Moses coming down from Sinai with a set of goals chiseled in stone. Instead, confer with your staff, letting the people who must meet the goals share in setting them. When you let staffers share in the planning, you tell them that you respect them — even those who think and react differently from you. As you work with them, remember the differences in behavior style and deal with individuals accordingly.

Do not attack a staffer's self-esteem, regardless of the behavior style the staffer follows. Ideas can be criticized. Actions can be criticized. But an individual's character and integrity should be respected. If you try to make subordinates look small, you're going to have an angry, bitter staff on your hands.

Eliminate the Negative

The wise coach will try to give positive, not negative, direction. Let people know that you expect the best of them. Staffers try to live up to your expectations. The negative-thinking coach might say to an assistant, "Why haven't you got those infielders in shape? They seem to be playing with holes in their gloves." The positive-thinking coach would say, "Let's talk about some ways we can tighten up our infield. You got any ideas?"

Delegate

Your staff members can't feel like winners if you're always the doer and they're always the go-fers. Be willing to delegate important tasks to them, always considering the characteristics of each behavior style. If it's a job that requires the staffer to spend lonely hours of study and concentration, don't delegate it to the sociable I person. The C is probably your best choice. If it's a job that requires delicate diplomacy, don't delegate it to the blunt D staffer. Your people-pleasing S is your best choice. If it's a job requiring firm discipline, don't delegate to assistants S or I. They dislike conflict and they fear being disliked. If it's a rush job that needs to be done immediately, don't go to your Cs. They won't turn it loose until they've checked and rechecked the dot on every "i" and the cross on every "t". Give the job to an I. If you have a task that involves long-range planning, trust your D.

Share the Sacrifices

Winning coaches set the examples for their staffs. When sacrifices are required, show that you're willing to share the burden. If the administration cuts the budget and you're not allowed to replace the assistant who left for greener pastures, don't put all the extra work on your subordinates. Show them that you're willing to pick up your share of the slack.

Once you've displayed that willingness, you're in better position to ask your staff to make sacrifices. If you're willing to give up a few evenings to practice the team, you won't have to apologize to your subordinates for asking them to make extra effort.

Let Staffers be Agents

Winning coaches don't treat their staffs like robots. They let them be agents who can think for themselves. Assistant coaches shouldn't have to tell the players, "Coach says you've gotta do this..." They should be able to give instructions on their own authority, subject to the general policies you set.

If your staffers are to be your agents, they need to know

your expectations. Tell them as clearly and unambiguously as you know how. Don't assume they already know what you want them to do and how you want them to act. Subordinates need to know what standards you use in making judgments. When you disagree with their judgments, tell them, diplomatically but clearly.

Listen to Objections

If your assistants have objections to some of your policies, listen to them. Even the best coaches make mistakes. The subordinate who is not afraid to voice objections may save you from embarrassing — and game-losing — errors.

You don't have to share the decision-making. The final call is yours to make. But it is good to let them know why you made a decision. Even if they don't agree with you, they will know your rationale.

Hold Gripe Sessions

Winning coaches know how to deal with hostility or dissatisfaction.

One way to get problems into the open is to hold "gripe sessions" with the staff. This isn't the kind of stress-producing session in which subordinates share grievances with no prospects of resolving them. It's a session in which you say to your staff, "I want you to tell me what's bugging you so that we can work together to do something about it."

It's best to hold these sessions around a table — preferably a round table — where everyone can be comfortable and nobody occupies the "head" position. You sit down with them as a participant rather than as the boss.

Let your staffers do the talking. This is not the place for the coach to dust off his or her D behavior style. But be responsive. When someone asks you a question, or looks to you for a response, paraphrase what has been said, then make your reply. That will show them that you're involved, that you've been paying attention.

Take notes on what is being said. That will tell your staffers you are genuinely interested in what they're saying and will indicate to them that you intend to do something about the things discussed. Another way to demonstrate your interest is to ask for details, especially in cases of complaints.

Using a flipchart or blackboard can open up the comments. The blank paper or board practically demands that someone say something to fill the space. Tell the staff, "Okay, we're going to put down some points to discuss. Just throw out anything that's on your mind...."

As you write down the points, keep your back to the group. People are more comfortable speaking their minds when they're not looking the boss in the eye.

At the end of the session, review the notes you've taken to make sure you've understood everything correctly.

Then follow through. Look into the things that need to be investigated, carry out the actions you've promised to carry out and report back to the people concerned. This will establish your credibility.

Be Sensitive

Hostility often arises because the boss is insensitive. North Carolina behavior scientists Morgan W. McCall and Michael M. Lombardo studied the cases of 21 executives whose careers had gotten off track. They found that the most frequent personality flaw was insensitivity to others.

If you want to avoid hostility on the part of your subordinates, be aware of their sensitive areas. Other people have egos too. You may think Assistant Coach Duncan is all ego, but remember that D people's egos propel them, and the team, toward victory. You may think Assistant Coach Irvin is a glory hound. But remember that for the I person, pressure time is opportunity time. You may think Assistant Coach Carson is a prickly know-it-all. But remember, the C person's eye for detail and passion for perfection is what polishes your team's execution. Even the passive Assistant Coach Simpson, a high S, has an ego that needs occasional stroking.

So give your subordinates recognition when they need it. Look for opportunities to praise them. Don't demean them when they're looking for support. Make conscious efforts to elevate their self-esteem.

Identify the Buttons

Everyone has certain buttons you don't want to push. Find out where your subordinates' sensitivities lie, and avoid irritating them unnecessarily. Never assume that a relationship is secure and will endure without further attention. All relationships need to be nurtured continually.

Avoid the words that anger and upset your staffers. This doesn't mean you have to avoid unpleasant subjects. Sometimes it's necessary to critique a staffer's performance and to point out areas that need improving. In such cases, lay the groundwork for what is coming. Explain to the person you're approaching what you're about to do and why you're about to do it.

When you do make someone angry, don't let the anger smolder. Take action quickly to defuse the anger. It need not be an apology; it may just be an acknowledgement: "You're angry at me, aren't you?" This at least opens the door for further conversation that could lead to a better understanding.

Invite Bad News

Winning coaches want their subordinates to come to them with the bad news. It isn't enough to tell them that. You have to demonstrate that you can handle it.

Here's where an easy, relaxed relationship with subordinates comes in handy. Coaches who regard themselves as lofty eminences, approachable only under the proper circumstances and at the proper time, will get little bad news from their subordinates. No one will want to break the news that the monarch is parading in public without a stitch of clothing on the royal frame. Your staffers will keep the bad news hidden until they've had a chance to fix what's wrong or bury what can't be fixed. They may not be afraid of you—it's just that by remaining remote from them you're saying to them, "Don't bother me with problems; I have more important things to think about."

You encourage the free flow of information — good and bad — by remaining available to your staff at all times and by getting out of your office and mingling with them.

Ask them questions. Not vague and general questions such as, "How are things going?" Ask a meaningless question like that and you'll get a meaningless answer: "Okay. How're things with you?"

Make your questions specific, with the objective of obtaining specific information: "How's Ted doing on those new pass patterns?" "Will the new uniforms be ready in time for the Homecoming game?" "Is Delores going to be ready to step in as center when we play Eastern State?"

Help With Solutions

Subordinates may be reluctant to bring their problems to you unless they have already worked out a solution that needs only your approval or disapproval. It's certainly a good idea to discourage your staff from delegating their work to you. But as head coach, you have knowledge, experience and perspective that can accelerate problem-solving. You need to share that with subordinates when the occasion arises.

Before saying to a subordinate, "That's your problem; go solve it," why not take the time to discuss it? Then decide whether it's something that needs your direct involvement or something that can be delegated.

Don't blame the bearer of bad news. Your staffers will keep you better informed if they know the news they bring you won't provoke your rage. It's a good idea to thank them for letting you know, and commend them for alerting you in time to avert disaster.

The Winning Chemistry

Finally, winning coaches build team chemistry.

As one former Green Bay Packer put it, "We got to be Lombardi people; we would only respond to his kind of coaching" (Dowling, 1970, p. 71).

You build that kind of chemistry by establishing a set of values that present and future members of your team can embrace.

When you evaluate people for promotion, or when you're hiring new talent, look for more than raw ability. Look for the candidate who fits the chemistry. Remember how the Lakers stuck with the modest, easygoing James Worthy instead of trading him for the more peppery Mark Aguirre? It wasn't a question of which person was the better athlete; it was a question of which best suited the team chemistry. A person who fit in well with the old St. Louis Cardinals' Gashouse Gang might have been a dud with the Yankees' Murderer's Row.

Intuition certainly plays a role in such choices. But an instrument such as the Performax Personal Profile System can identify a candidate's behavior style. A knowledge of these behavior styles can help you define the qualities that make an individual compatible or incompatible with the team's chemistry — and yours.

THE FIVE Ls

At a seminar on mental health, Dr. Barrie Greiff, a psychiatrist who taught at Harvard Business School, summed up his formula for successful living with the Five Ls. They are the capacities to love, learn, labor, laugh and leave. Effective coaches will seek to cultivate them in themselves and in their subordinates.

By "love," we don't mean romantic love or the touchy-feely variety. We mean a genuine concern for others, in the spirit of the Golden Rule. That kind of love motivates the staffer to put out the extra effort to help individuals and to help the team. The coach should be the prime exemplar of this type of concern.

The capacity to learn requires an open mind. The coach who is willing to listen and learn from assistants and players provides encouragement for subordinates to do likewise.

Labor lies behind every achievement. A brilliant idea may spring out of thin air, but it takes effort to implement the idea. And the idea provides no lasting satisfaction until it has been converted to reality. Then comes the reward. The winning coach helps subordinates reap this satisfaction by providing an environment that encourages productive labor.

Laughter is a pleasant lubricant for life. The ability to laugh at oneself as well as with others softens adversity and bolsters morale so that the adversity can be conquered.

The capacity to leave may seem to be a strange companion to the other capacities. Yet it is important. Nothing is permanent. There comes a time when departures are necessary. People move on to greater challenges; people find it easier to move than to adapt to new circumstances; family situations change; people die.

We all must have the capacity to leave old situations and move on to new ones.

Jerry West was Pat Riley's closest friend when they were teammates on the Los Angeles Lakers. West later became general manager of the Lakers, while Riley became the coach.

One day, West talked to Riley about the conflict between personal loyalty and the need to keep the team competitive: "You know, there might come a day when I have to fire you," West told his friend.

"I understand that," said Riley. "And there might come a day when I decide to walk away from the team" (Riley, 1988, p. 42).

Both smiled. Both remained friends. Each was loyal to the Lakers. Each cared about the individuals in the organization. But each had the capacity to leave. In time, Riley left.

THE GAME OF LIFE

Athletic banquet speakers down through the years have belabored the analogy between the sports contest and the "game of life." The analogy is apt in many respects, but the athlete and the coach need to understand that it is just an analogy. The game is not life—at least it isn't all there is to life.

In most athletic events, for one side to win the other side must lose. That's not necessarily true in life. We all can be winners without making losers of those around us. In fact, the big winners in life are those who help others become winners. It may seem strange to end a book about coaches and winning by referring to the Golden Rule, but the Golden Rule is an important element in the winning style.

"No man is an island," wrote John Donne, who would have included both genders in his phraseology had he written at the close of the 20th century.

Whether it's Martina Navratilova pursuing a singles victory on the tennis court, or Diana Nyad battling the chops in the English Channel, or Joe Montana passing for a touchdown, or Orel Hershiser pitching a shutout, or Tommy Lasorda pacing the dugout, victory is not a single-handed achievement. Even when the winning performance is an individual act, it arises from an elaborate groundwork of support — from coaches, trainers, colleagues, friends and family. The individual cannot win unless members of the group become winners.

The successful person — in the athletic arena or the arena of life — can succeed only by making it possible for others to succeed.

That's why we need to know what motivates others, what gratifies them, what hurts them and what demoralizes them. We achieve that knowledge by learning their behavior styles. We turn that knowledge into a formula for victory by applying it in the light of the Golden Rule. We learn how others want to be treated. Then we try, to the best of our ability and circumstances, to treat them that way. The coach who follows this formula is the coach who knows how to win with style.

Epilogue

The behavior styles used in this book are those identified through the Personal Profile System, copyright (1990) by Performax Systems International, Inc.

The author has used this system successfully in workshops with coaches and teams.

The PPS system is available through the author. Those wishing to obtain it or to inquire about a workshop, presentation or consultation may write:

    Kay McGuire
    Center for Creative Communication
    7 Dunlap Court
    Savoy, IL 61874

References

Alessandra, Tony, and Michael J. O'Connor. 1990. *People Smart: Powerful Techniques for Turning Every Encounter into a Mutual Win.* With Janice Alessandra. La Jolla, CA: Keynote Publishing.

Benson, Hebert. 1975. *The Relaxation Response.* New York: William Morrow.

Bouton, Jim, ed. 1973. *I Managed Good, But Boy Did They Play Bad.* With Neil Offen. Chicago: Playboy Press.

Bouton, Jim. 1973a. "A Locker Room View." In Bouton, ed., *I Managed Good, But Boy Did They Play Bad.* Chicago: Playboy Press.

Bouton, Jim. 1973b. Introduction. *I Managed Good, But Boy Did They Play Bad.* By Bouton, ed. Chicago: Playboy Press.

Creamer, Robert W. 1974. *Babe: The Legend Comes to Life.* New York: Simon & Schuster.

Dowling, Tom. 1970. *Coach: A Season With Lombardi.* New York: Popular Library, by arrangement with W. W. Norton.

Evans, Richard. 1982. *McEnroe: A Rage for Perfection.* In cooperation with John McEnroe. New York: Simon & Schuster.

Fitzgerald, Ed. 1973. "Nobody's Neutral." In Bouton, ed., *I Managed Good, But Boy Did They Play Bad.* Chicago: Playboy Press.

Jackson, Reggie. 1984. *Reggie: the Autobiography.* With Mike Lupica. New York: Villard Books.

Krugel, Mitchell. 1989. *Michael Jordan.* New York: St. Martin's Press.

Linn, Edward. 1973. "The Last Angry Old Man." In Bouton, ed., *I Managed Good, But Boy Did They Play Bad.* Chicago: Playboy Press.

Martin, Billy. 1987. *Billyball.* With Phil Pepe. Garden City, NY: Doubleday.

Mays, Willie. 1988. *Say Hey: The Autobiography of Willie Mays.* With Lou Sahadi. New York: Simon & Schuster.

Mellen, Joan. 1989. *Bob Knight, His Own Man.* New York: Avon Books.

Nyad, Diana. 1978. *Other Shores.* New York: Random House.

Paterno, Joe. 1989. *Paterno: By the Book.* With Bernard Asbell. New York: Random House.

Perkins, Bill. 1989. *Kids in Sports.* With Rod Cooper. Portland, OR: Multinomah Press.

Plimpton, George. 1974. *Hank Aaron: One for the Record.* New York: Bantam Books.

The Research Institute of America. 1986. *Creating and Motivating a Superior, Loyal Staff.* New York: RIA.

Retton, Mary Lou, and Bela Karolyi. 1986. *Mary Lou: Creating an Olympic Champion.* With John Powers. New York: McGraw-Hill.

Riley, Pat. 1988. *Show Time: Inside the Lakers' Breakthrough Season.* New York: Warner Books.

Rose, Pete. 1970. *The Pete Rose Story: An Autobiography.* Cleveland: World Publishing.

Schembechler, Bo, and Mitch Albom. 1989. *Bo.* New York: Warner Books.

Seidel, Michael. 1988. *Streak: Joe DiMaggio and the Summer of 1941.* New York: McGraw-Hill.

Stamborski, Jim. 1988. *Don't Get Me Wrong.* Chicago: Chicago Review Press.

Temple, Ed. 1980. *Only the Pure in Heart Survive.* With B'Lou Carter. Nashville, TN: Broadman Press.

Thorn, John. 1976. *A Century of Baseball Lore.* New York: Hart Publishing.

Veeck, Bill. 1973. "Which of Us Took the Greater Fall?" In Bouton, ed., *I Managed Good, But Boy Did They Play Bad.* Chicago: Playboy Press.